Shadow over Fiji

Shadow over Fiji

A Memoir

Barbara Restle

VANTAGE PRESS
New York

Although this is a true story, all names
have been changed to protect the privacy
of the innocent and not so innocent.

FIRST EDITION

All rights reserved, including the right of
reproduction in whole or in part in any form.

Copyright © 1999 by Barbara Restle

Published by Vantage Press, Inc.
516 West 34th Street, New York, New York 10001

Manufactured in the United States of America
ISBN: 0-533-13069-7

Library of Congress Catalog Card No.: 99-93570

0 9 8 7 6 5 4 3 2 1

To my children: Andrea, Kathleen, and Phillip

"We have a world outside us, a universe within."
—J. Heap

Contents

Preface ix
Acknowledgment xi

1. Chief Siti — 1
2. One Down—Twenty to Go — 11
3. Where in Tarnation Is Beni? — 25
4. Bats in the Vale Lailai — 32
5. Don't Bulls Have Rights, Too? — 40
6. Who's in Charge Anyway? — 50
7. Liku — 57
8. Akariva versus Constructive Ambiguities — 68
9. Too Many Babies and No Calves — 83
10. Cultural Conundrum? — 99
11. Grand Pacific Hotel — 110
12. The Hungarian and the U.S. Embassy Lady — 119
13. Home Sweet *Bure* — 143
14. Lasa — 148
15. Dr. Tomba — 169
16. Fortitude or Folly? — 180
17. A Desk Job — 192
18. Timoci — 198
19. The Future—An Unwelcome Guest — 205
20. The Ancients Come Knocking — 217

Epilogue — 225

Preface

We are all motivated to reach a point of involvement that insures protection. And the goal we set ourselves to protect . . . ?

Acknowledgment

I wish to acknowledge and thank Jeanne Meyers, on the staff of Indiana University, for providing invaluable help to me in preparing my manuscript for publication.

Shadow over Fiji

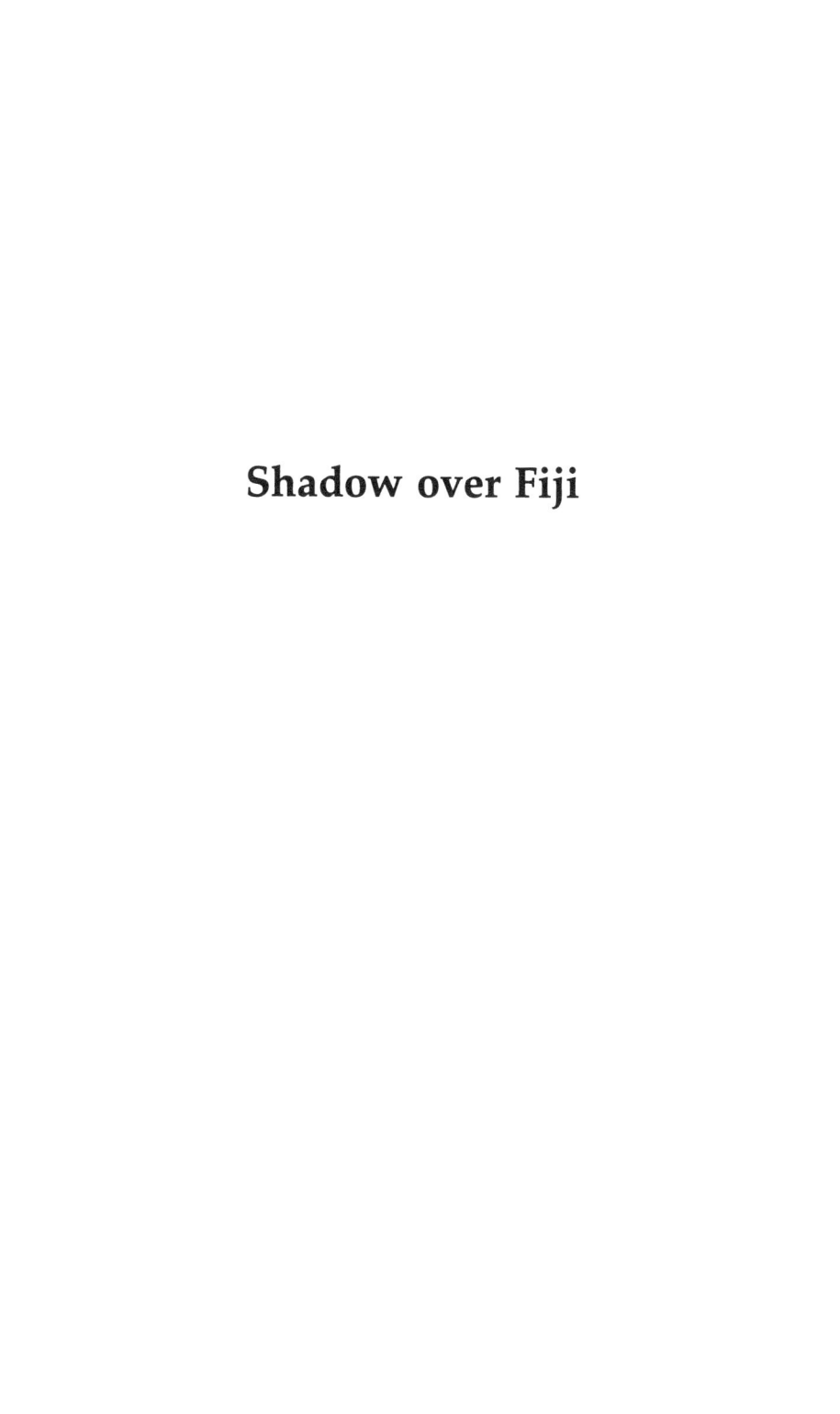

1
Chief Siti

In the chief's bamboo *bure* in a remote village in Fiji, my perfect record for holding my grog was shattered forever. On my arrival at the cattle scheme Chief Siti and his elders had invited me to a welcoming *yanqona* drinking ceremony.

The ruinous ending to this ancient traditional ritual was to haunt me during my entire eighteen months' work as livestock officer. By the ubiquitous jungle grapevine, news of the event reached surrounding villages and eventually my HQ in Suva, the capital city. Several months later I had good reason to wonder if this one disastrous afternoon in Chief Siti's *bure* did not give a man, a man watching me with more than benign curiosity, reason to categorize me as a vulnerable and muddle-headed woman. This man, a Fijian called Beni, was the livestock officer in charge of the 3,000-acre cattle scheme with 500 cattle in residence. We were to work together as a team. I was to learn in the hardest way possible that Beni had every reason in his work to see me gone from this cattle scheme. The mere absence of Beni from my welcoming party should have alerted me to something being seriously amiss.

The ceremonial welcoming for me began with a solemn meeting in Chief Siti's large bamboo *bure,* his home.

Chief Siti, his grown sons, and a dozen village elders sat cross-legged around the huge hand-carved wooden bowl, the village *tanoa*. I sat facing Chief Siti, a place of honor, wearing baggy new jeans and a white shirt. The men wore their *sulus*, knee-length skirts wrapped around their waists, clean but work-worn. In the afternoon heat of a tropical summer the men's bare upper bodies glistened blue-black and were covered with oily sweat. The air inside this windowless round hut was heavy with moisture. No breeze squeezed through the tightly plaited bamboo walls and thatch roof.

The only woman other than myself was the chief's wife, Zeta. When I first arrived she motioned me to take off my sandals, leave them outside, and dip my feet in a bucket of water. Zeta hovered on her knees near the entrance to her home and did not join us in our circle around the *tanoa*. When Zeta saw the ceaseless biting flies had found me she moved gracefully on her knees to place a small plaited grass fan beside me and quickly withdrew to a corner. During the long afternoon she never spoke or moved again.

The tall, muscular Chief Siti mumbled his lengthy welcome in the local dialect, his eyes focused on the empty three-legged wooden bowl before him. To me his language was meaningless. One month's intensive language schooling did not include bush dialects in mumbles.

Kona, the chief's oldest son, a handsome sixteen-year-old, sat next to his father, also pondering the wooden bowl. When his father finished Kona rose on his knees and moved toward me.

He whispered in perfect English, "Miss Barbara, it is now time to give your present, your *sevu sevu*, to my father."

On my knees I moved slowly toward the chief. Kona intercepted me and held out both his hands to receive my newspaper-wrapped bundle of *yanqona* roots. Chief Siti's second-eldest son, also on his knees, took the *yanqona* from Kona. How gracefully the men walked on their knees. For some reason the sons didn't want me too close to their father. Still on my knees I returned to my place and found Kona was now sitting beside me.

Chief Siti's ancestors had belonged to a warrior tribe, and he looked the role with his sculpted face and every move studied, economical. He didn't look into my face, and his mask of indifference never altered. None of the men, elders or sons, made eye contact with one another or with me. I looked at Zeta and found her eyes focused on her husband's feet. I also concentrated on not looking into the eyes of the chief. In orientation lectures I had learned making eye contact was a cultural signal of aggression or sexual interest in Fiji. Did this mean I might look at any other body part? All the men found my bare feet fascinating to gaze upon. I also rested my eyes on the chief's large calloused black feet. A furtive glance found the shade of his hair was not the same color as the tightly frizzed black hair of the other men. Kona's hair was, like his father's, a dark rust color.

Kona whispered in English, "Our *yanqona tanoa* bowl is the largest in Fiji. It is a village treasure. The bowl was carved by our ancestors from a tree maybe four hundred years old. Even the oldest man in our village, born during the years of tribal wars, does not know how old our *tanoa* is."

Back home in the Midwest the bowl might serve a punch party of a hundred or more without refilling. It was the same size as a tub I had used many years ago to bathe my babies.

Chief Siti placed both his hands on the package of *yanqona* and, speaking to the wooden bowl, finished his dialogue and mumbled several times, "*Vanaka vaka levu*, Miss

Barbara," which I finally understood as a "thank you very much, Miss Barbara."

Chief Siti's second-eldest son poured water from a dented metal wash bucket into the bowl and wrapped the *yanqona* in a cloth bag that looked like a worn-out cotton sock. I saw with relief that the bucket I had used for my dirty feet was still in place outside the open door. The chief's son patiently kneaded the roots until the water was the same shade as the silt-laden, mustard-colored stream outside the *bure*. Then the serious drinking ceremony began.

For the next three hours I sat on the handwoven *imbe*, the grass mat laid on top of the floor of hard-packed clay. At the end of one hour a creeping numbness in my hips and legs replaced nagging muscle cramps. There was no chair in sight, but lots of pillows on beds against the walls. My eyes went to the pillows as I willed Zeta to bring me some to sit on. But her eyes never left her husband's feet. I tried kneeling, but soon my knees turned to concrete. I tried sitting with my legs straight out in front, but my lumber spine went into spasms. At the end of two hours and after many coconut shells of *yanqona*, a generalized numbness replaced all cramps and spasms and I was feeling relaxed. I enjoyed a lovely sensation of floating slightly above the woven grass mat. My arms and legs grew long and rubbery, and I was at peace in my new world.

The correct way to drink *yanqona* in a ceremony is by putting the coconut shell to your lips and drinking until the shell is drained. With the first swallow of the vile, bitter, muddy brew my face involuntarily skewed, my eyes clenched shut. I drank the grainy liquid, and it was not like anything my lips had ever tasted. If lime, alum, sand, and muddy creek water were joined together in a blender, they would taste like *yanqona*. "Here's mud in your eye" must have originated with the colonial Brits drinking the *yanqona* grog cocktail of choice when visiting a Fijian village.

After drinking from the coconut shells, the men placed their shells on the mat and clapped three times. Most of the men grimaced when swallowing the grog. If no one liked the vile brew, why did they drink it?

At some point after ten coconut bowls I lost count. Big mistake. Each round was followed by more hands clapping three times.

This grog was described to me by Fijian language teachers as an hallucinogen. How much was too much? All the Fijians just shrugged a "who knows?" Was it like five beers or three martinis, definitely too much during a lunch break? More shrugs.

With every coconut bowl successfully drained honoring me as the new *bulamacow* livestock officer my confidence grew. I was playing my part without a hitch. *Bring on all your hungry and sick cows. I'm ready to save your cattle scheme,* I thought bravely. This cattle operation was not going to go belly-up like the one managed by the fundamentalist Christian church of whatever denomination, in the other agricultural district. Yes indeed, I could fit into this thousand-year-old—or was it two-thousand-year-old—black culture! Not only could I drink and keep up with a 225-pound warrior chief and his village elders, but I was also beginning to make sense of their mumbled dialect. The brew was easier to swallow with each round.

The brew with its bitter, face-wrenching taste somehow became nothing more than a grainy brown liquid. My lips were heavy, puffy tissue somewhere on the lower part of my face. At some point during the last hour of the ceremony my face was replaced by a numb wooden mask. My swollen velvet tongue mumbled fluent Fijian in the local dialect. Finding it hard to move a tongue around that did not quite fit in my mouth, I nevertheless made polite Fijian conversation, with endless *"vanaka vaka levus"*—thank you very much.

When Kona nudged me indicating the conclusion of the welcoming ceremony, I wondered why we had to end this pleasant little afternoon. I tried to rise. In my extended cramped sitting position my legs had lost all life. My rubber arms couldn't help me to rise. Somewhere below my waist I had ceased to exist. I wondered if I might just curl up on the *imbe* and go to sleep. My body floated on a soft, grassy mattress, and I never wanted to leave.

I stood up or rather tried but stumbled and fell straightaway into the holy and revered *tanoa* bowl. Kona jumped to my side to right me, but not before one of my bare feet stood in a puddle of the brown liquid remaining in the ceremonial bowl.

I stared at my foot and saw brown wet dregs of the grog seeping between my toes. My foot seemed miles below me and heavy as lead. Stern black faces encircled me, and I saw black eyes angrily meeting mine. What I had done was the symbolic equivalent of a rebel washing her dirty feet in the baptismal fountain of a Christian church. Chief Siti, a glowering six-foot-tall warrior monument, stood before me. He looked directly into my eyes with the most compelling message of aggression.

In perfect textbook Fijian he said, "For this insult to us we have killed in the past."

The chief and the elders turned their backs on me and left the *bure*.

Kona, still holding my arm, said, "No one ever has done this to our *tanoa*. My father is very angry."

Dazed, I looked Kona in the eyes and through lips strangely lazy replied, "I thoroughly enjoyed my welcoming party honoring my arrival in your village. We might do this again, but next time, Kona, you will have to find me a chair."

Actually these were my intended words, but my lips wouldn't honor the message sent via a bundle of nerves from the *yanqona*-saturated brain, and neither would the tongue.

I had never abused drugs. This was a first. A disappointed Kona wobbled before my dilated pupils. *Interesting*, I told myself, because I was still clear-headed. Was I not thinking logically? I will never know. If you ask a falling-down drunk if he is fully capable of functioning will he tell the real truth or the truth as he sees it? *Yanqona* is an hallucinogenic drug. The only truth I was capable of stating was that I was not hallucinating. Or was I?

Zeta took my arm and gently led me to a small *bure*, showed me to my own airfoam mattress, and helped me lie down. She carefully tucked the mosquito netting under the mattress. I was behind a lovely white wedding veil. Like on my wedding day. What a charming scene. Through my veil I watched Zeta holding a small, flickering kerosene lamp. Was it night already? She whispered, "*So mothe*, Miss Barbara, *so mothe*," good night.

* * *

Only the next morning did I comprehend the extent of my image problem. Kona patiently and kindly explained to me that if a Fijian had done this deed his throat might have been cut. If not in his *bure*, then later in the bush in the night. Kona added that his father and the elders had conferred in the night and agreed to assign him, Kona, to watch over me and protect me. They knew not from what.

Kona said, "This morning the oldest of the village fathers believe if you are not possessed by spirits then what?

He saw this very morning a bantam rooster here in the village lay a spotted egg."

"All because I lost my balance last night."

"Miss Barbara, there is more, the village fathers have decided."

Kona hesitated before continuing. His mouth turned up at the corners but barely perceptibly. His handsome young face averted from mine, he said, "My grandfather, who was chief of this village before my father, is going to adopt you as his daughter."

I tried to control my instant anger. If I was to manage this cattle scheme that had at this time taken more than $125,000 of World Bank money, I needed all the respect I could command. I was to be adopted by the old village chief? I didn't want an old man holding my hand, acting as my protector. Was it one step up or one step down from being appointed wife number two or three?

"If this is what it takes for me to inspect my first farm," I finally said to Kona, "then for the sake of five hundred cows let's get one more meeting over with as soon as possible."

"I'll walk you up to your *bure* now, help you carry your bedroll and everything else. Soon we'll go on to my grandfather's *bure.* He is expecting you. You will have to take a package of *yanqona* for the adoption ceremony."

Before Kona made his hasty exit his face broke into an ear-to-ear grin. I groaned and slumped back down on my cot. One more *yanqona* ceremony!

The children of the village giggled when they saw me go to the *vale lailai,* "house little," the outhouse. I vowed never to buy *yanqona* from that Indian in the city again. It was the Indian's fault. He had sold me a highly potent variety. Maybe he had laced it with something. Just like the days of prohibition in the States, there was no standardization. Every package bought was a *caveat emptor* purchase.

The first rule I learned in my language classes in this country was that whenever one looked for the cause of a fault, any fault, one should focus immediately on the Indian. My Fijian language teachers blamed the Indian for being, among many other sins, greedy, and my Indian language teachers blamed Fijians for being lazy, along with many other accompanying sins. When you are living in a Fijian village everything bad that happens is supposedly the fault of the 48 percent Indian population who mostly lived in cities. When living with an Indian family one learns to blame everything bad on the 50 percent Fijians who mostly lived in villages. Now that I was part of only a 2 percent white population I was feeling an angst entirely new to me. It was easy in this culture to blame failures on the Fijian or the Indian culture. But if I was to get my work done the race question must remain a moot point.

There was an immense amount of work to complete in a short time. Two problems were obvious. One agricultural officer said the cattle scheme had used more than the $125,000 grant deposited in the Suva bank. Another officer said the entire $200,000 grant had been spent. Did the real truth matter if the 500 cattle were in poor condition? There were twenty-one farms, twenty-one Fijian farmers with loans to pay off at the Suva bank. The loans were not being paid off in the allotted period of time, and the question was, Why?

I planned to visit at least one farm a day five days a week. The walking was going to be the hardest part of the job. *Over hill and dale in this country*, I thought smiling skeptically, was going to be a scramble up and down hills on hands and knees. If 3,000 acres of hills were flattened, how many acres would that be? Before I left my Midwest home, I had asked a geologist friend that question. He had looked at a topomap of Fiji and glumly said he didn't have the heart to tell me.

2
One Down—Twenty to Go

My small but new woven bamboo *bure* sat on top of a high grass-covered hill with a 360-degree vista. Not a tree or a shrub sheltered it. The square-built hut, exposed and vulnerable to the capricious tropical weather systems, had a certain jaunty presence. This was typhoon-prone land. Maybe the winds would find their way through the cracks of the woven bamboo walls and not blow my *bure* off its hilltop.

Surrounding dark green undulating hills were far away on the horizon. About five hundred feet below me. I could just see a *bure* through branches of heavy bush. This was the home of my only neighbors for a mile in all directions.

A corrugated tin roof lay more or less flat on my home, to complement four walls only slightly askew. There were three doors made of rough planks of wood and one window with a shutter that dropped down. Privacy is never a priority in Fiji; when one closes the doors and windows, wide gaps between rough boards and woven bamboo will give full view to the inside.

Standing inside my new home, I quickly forgot its precarious location. It was cozy and welcoming and clean. Sunlight filtered through the woven bamboo cast a cheery golden glow on walls and new grass floor mats. I have always loved, even craved, quiet places. No unwelcome noises invaded this space. Later that night, tucked under my new mosquito net, I fell asleep listening to distant mooing. Good, my neighbors had at least one cow—maybe this was one of the twenty-one farms I was to visit and report on.

The floor of my hut was hard-packed clay covered with woven grass *imbe* mats laid on top of woven bamboo. The soft mats were comforting to my bare feet. House cleaning meant shaking out the *imbe*. My airfoam mattress lay on a wood plank platform built so that the planks could be removed to hold my books and keep them out of harm's way from typhoon-driven rain. I tried not to think about how to keep myself dry when wind-whipped rain leaked through bamboo and under the tin roof. Large ragged spaces between the roof and walls would be nice for ventilation as well as mosquitoes.

There was no furniture, but I had a wood plank counter on which to put my wick cooking stove, my Coleman stove, and a few dishes and pots. A tiny aluminum sink sat on top of this counter, with a lead drain pipe leading down to the clay floor, outside the walls, and down a steep hillside. Nice to know I would never have plumbing problems. By bedtime I was to learn that water was a major problem. In a region with 200 inches of rain a year I was never to have enough water. I had been told earlier that boiling all drinking water was a must. I found two dented rusty buckets by the open back door. Peering around outside, I saw no evidence of a stream or a water cistern. One bucket for my bath and the other for cooking and drinking was to be my daily ration. *Sa oti!* That's it! If I wanted any more, obviously I had to get the water myself. But from where?

My expectations were always realistic. As I was working in a third world nation, allowances would have to be made. But no showers, no plumbing whatsoever, this was going to be a test of endurance. Where was that bucket shower contraption Nelly Forbush used in the musical *South Pacific* when she washed that man out of her hair? She didn't have any plumbing, either. Well, my children had hiked and camped in the wilderness of the Rockies for a month and survived and loved it. Without their tough mom they never would have attempted that challenge.

Close by my hut I had a new *vale lailai,* which I didn't have to share with anyone. It was built with three woven bamboo walls, the entrance covered with a faded and fraying curtain that had a tendency to lift high in the slightest breeze. Inside I gratefully found a concrete toilet, with no seat but what looked like a sturdy floor made of coconut tree logs. Most villages did not have this level of luxury.

My neighboring family, Maria and Tomaci and their seven children, lived in a *bure* larger than mine but in poor repair and smoke-blackened. Kerosene for cook stoves took money, so all their cooking was done over a wood fire, and during the long winter rainy season that meant cooking inside. They had no furniture and no sink. Clothing for Sunday going to church was kept in cardboard suitcases. The family slept on *imbe* rolled up in the morning and piled up against the walls. No one in the family used a pillow.

During my year living in the bush I slowly became part of Maria and Tomaci's family. They watched my every move. If they had a message for me or brought me a snack, they waited until my bathtowel was thrown over a laundry line to dry. That meant I was finished working for the day and decent for a visit.

Maria and her husband were the same age as I was, but when they told me to do something I never questioned why. Often I had no clue to their reasoning. One evening, two months after my arrival, Maria knocked on my door and announced herself. Always before she had sent one of her children to give me a message. Even by a weak kerosene lamp I clearly saw a worried Maria. She repeated the words, *"Ca bogi, ca bogi,"* emphasizing the fact that the night is a bad time. She asked me to keep my lamp lit all night, every night. I had never done that before because I had to carry kerosene several miles into the bush. But without questioning her I did what she asked. Thereafter, every night the burning wick turned low in my lamp gave a weak, flickering light until I closed it down at dawn. When I went to my *vale lailai* before bed I saw that even this tiny flame could be seen through the slits of the woven bamboo walls of my hut. After I moved into town, I found Maria in all likelihood had saved my life in the bush.

The couple's youngest daughter, eleven-year-old Ili, was designated my water carrier. Every day after school she brought two buckets to my front door. Shy and quiet, Ili put down the buckets, smiled at me, and quickly ran back down the path to her *bure*. Only after several weeks of my giving her a cookie or some candy did Ili finally stay to chat, giving me news of her day in school. Fijian mothers bring up their daughters with the knowledge that there is a "queen residing" within their heads. Watching Ili walking to school, her back straight, her head high, barefoot in all weather, I saw an elegant young girl. Years later when she became a wife and subservient to her man, she would be comforted by knowing there was "queen within."

My first order of business after moving into my new home was to thumbtack shelving paper on the bush timber holding up my walls, sketch a rough map of the cattle scheme, and draw in the approximate locations of twenty-one farms. The cattle scheme was in the shape of an eggplant, with my *bure* in the center. All twenty-one farmers had family names with at times five syllables, names impossible for me to memorize, so I gave them initials and numbers and kept a list of their actual names also thumbtacked to a beam.

With one farm inspection a day and an extra one thrown in on an easy day the first reports should be completed within a month, I thought confidently.

My first site visit began on the farm of Virimi, the son of eighty-year-old Orisi, the retired chief who had adopted me as his daughter. The morning after the welcoming ceremony that had created my *yanqona* hangover, I finally understood why Orisi was adopting me. Strategically he took me out of the category of stranger and identified me as a member of his family, and not just any family but a chiefly one. Family and stranger are the only two categories in Fiji. Orisi, a retired chief, guaranteed me status and safety. I was his daughter. Theoretically, no one dared touch me without risking his chiefly wrath. This also meant that his son Virimi was chiefly, a fact I must never forget.

Virimi's farm was one of broad sweeps of rolling green pastures. He had cleared timber on both shores of a shallow rocky stream that meandered through his farm. It was the same stream that several miles downhill gave me my two buckets of water every day. This was a cautionary: I drank the very water all his cattle walked in, drank from, and deposited their bovine brand of ammonia and nitrogen in.

Virimi was a serious middle-aged farmer. Sinewy and small-framed, he worked hard on his farm while never appearing hurried or overworked. The entire afternoon of my first visit, even when his gaze lingered on his cattle, a smile never softened his sharp features. His deepset eyes under a prominent brow never met mine. Obviously he considered himself chiefly, as was his father.

Virimi's cattle, white and all shades of brown, grazed in the valley bisected by the clear running stream. I would have liked to have seen the cattle carry more weight. Their breeding, a mix of Brahman and Hereford, was good—they were long-bodied, long-legged modern cows, but without enough muscle and no fat. They were not getting enough forage, not enough minerals. I saw no salt blocks, which in the United States cost only a couple of dollars each, but in this country I was to find that minerals were a luxury. Virimi and I walked into the heavily treed hills surrounding his farm. He wanted to show me how much hardwood timber he had to sell. We were looking at thousands of dollars' income and a catastrophe in the making.

"Virimi, if you cut all the trees on these hills you're going to lose topsoil and make deep ravines. Your cattle won't get good grass on these hills. They could also fall and break legs."

"Miss Barbara, I need the money from my trees."

"You need the right grasses, too. The nutritional value of your pastures is too low."

"To plant the good grasses I need money to get them and also time to improve the pastures. First I think I need to sell the timber."

"First you will have to sell some of your cows. They look healthy, but they are too thin. You don't have enough grass. You might also have a worm problem."

"Building a race, a corral, to confine them for treatment takes time and money."

"Virimi, not if several of you farmers work together. We're also going to have to test for TB and Brucellosis."

"Beni never asked us to test our cows."

"When was the last time Beni saw your cows?"

Virimi turned his head slightly away and focused on a faraway hill. His body language told me he didn't care to go on with this question-and-answer dialogue. I most certainly did.

Beni had been and still was the designated livestock officer in charge of this scheme and responsible for reporting and making recommendations. He and I were to work as a team. I had reason to believe he was avoiding me. True, I had been here only a week, but Beni had made no attempt to meet with me. Until I could study every bit of information he had gathered on this cattle scheme I had only my eyes to gather vital facts.

Virimi's lack of response to my questions I interpreted to mean, "You ask only rhetorical questions." I felt an unease with his closed-book approach. If his attitude represented the feelings of the other twenty men, I needed to confer with Beni as soon as possible.

"Virimi, you're telling me that none of your cattle have ever been tested for TB or *Brucellosis*?"

"Maybe before they came. I don't know. *Senga na lenga,* no problem, Miss Barbara."

That meant the cattle probably had tested negative before they were delivered, as in "maybe" or "we usually take this fact on faith." The first foreboding, the first fear, took residence in me. TB kills cattle and people, and Brucellosis makes both miserably sick.

"Virimi, information I have on your cows indicates you have six cows more than your bank says you have. Have you bought some recently?"

Virimi again turned his head and gazed off toward another set of hills. Every time I asked a question he didn't want to answer, he found another hill to examine. Fiji is nothing but hills, so this could go on for hours.

Virimi was giving me a lot of bad information by not giving me any. He was holding back. Where did Virimi get more than a thousand dollars to buy cows? Cows that he simply, as we say in the Midwest, did not have enough groceries to feed. More important, if he had that kind of money he should have been paying off his bank loan.

This was only my first site visit; therefore, patience was in order. There would be many more visits. I also needed to remain in his good graces, as well as his father's, as Orisi was my protection in my new job.

A year later I was to find out that Orisi had done his very best to keep me out of harm's way. He knew nothing about cattle management, but he knew why there were six cows in his son's herd for which I had no record. And he knew to whom those cows belonged. Orisi feared for my safety before he even set eyes on me. The only power he had he used in adopting me as his daughter and removing me from the category of a stranger.

Virimi's steady gaze toward the hills never wavered when I asked, "Where is your bull? You must have him secured somewhere."

"No bull here."

"How long has it been since you have no bull? I see a young calf nursing."

"My bull visiting farm some kilometers away. He helps himself as he will. He is Brahman, Indian. Just like Indian men in the city, he likes to visit all manner of cows."

"But you have a cow in estrus now. I saw her. You only have at most ten to twelve hours before she will not be receptive to the bull."

"*Senga na lenga,* no problem. Soon the winds in the evening will change. My bull will smell her signal and come home to her."

I laughed with gusto, releasing my anxiety. Another brand of jungle telephone in this land. When Suni, my local boss, wanted me to come to his agricultural station he sent word to the village schoolteacher, who was his neighbor. The next day the teacher told Ili to give me the message. When Ili brought me my two buckets of water in the evening she would tell me Suni wanted me in his office in the morning. The jungle telephone never failed to find a willing wavelength. Virimi's cow emitted a pheromone that traveled kilometers to an enthusiastic wandering bull with a robust olfactory sense. Interesting idea. If this was true for all Fijian bulls, this scheme didn't need many bulls.

We walked toward Virimi's home, and I saw his father, Orisi, plodding up the bush path from the direction of town. He was a walking inspiration. Leaning on his long staff, a small white dog cradled in his other arm, his spare body was bent almost ninety degrees. He trudged steadily up the hill with his eyes on the ground. If he wanted to see ahead of him, he had to turn his entire body a little sideways. Unlike most old men, he always wore a faint, secretive little smile, as if the world around him was exactly the way he wanted it to be.

Virimi, his wife Lena, Orisi, and I sat on the wooden deck attached to Virimi's home, which overlooked all his pastures. Pastures that I now knew grew all the wrong grasses. Plenty of roughage but little nutrition.

I saw Lena in her kitchen making tea. Rarely was I ever served real tea, an expensive brew. The women picked leaves from wild lemon trees growing in the bush. Unlike her husband, she didn't talk to me in English, but I knew she understood me. Her silence was her way of being subservient in front of the men. She was tall, a strong, healthy woman with a face so open and pleasant I relaxed in her presence. In Fijian she said she understood I was now

Orisi's adopted daughter. As she spoke she smiled broadly, clearly amused at my now being a sister to her. A month later, I was to find that as my sister she was obligated to weave me a new grass *imbe*, a very beautiful one. This one was to be my bedspread, too fine to walk on, and she fringed it with brightly colored wool.

Lena served all of us hot tea in chipped mugs before she settled herself leaning against the bamboo wall of her *bure*. We all gazed off into the surrounding hills. No one spoke. I was tired from hours of walking on rough terrain. And for the first time in weeks I didn't feel lonely. I was treated as family. I was accepted. These farmers understood I was weary. And they knew the value of a close family bonding. No need to talk about it or anything else. My thoughts went back to my farm report in my knapsack and those extra cows. I couldn't bring myself to intrude, to break into this intimate feeling of belonging, by asking a question that clearly made Virimi uncomfortable.

Orisi spoke not one word the entire time I was on Virimi's land. He merely glanced in my direction from time to time and smiled gently. His gnarled hands encircled his mug. With his advanced arthritis the hot mug probably felt good. His black skin was wrinkled in gray baggy ridges on his knees and ankles. With the bulk of his life behind him I marveled at his ready beatific smile. This farm of Virimi's was in all likelihood really Orisi's. When he was young he might not have had money to buy cattle. Borrowing from a bank was a new idea in Fiji. He might have grown *cassava* and *dalo* in his bottomlands. Maybe bananas. Virimi's cattle operation would be new to Orisi. I doubted if he knew anything about cattle diseases or what was needed to manage a thriving cattle herd. He was no longer the chief of the village near the main road but coming to the end of his days. What made this ancient man with his tortured spine so pleased to be alive? So generous to a white stranger?

I marveled at the lush and serene vista all around me. On the horizon stretched miles of green jungle, vigorous and untamed, a joy for one's eyes to caress from a distance but deadly to lose one's way within. I sat leaning against the *bure,* turned my face toward the cooling late-afternoon breeze, and closed my eyes. I was under a spell. With the peace, the friendly ease, I wanted to doze off. Is that what is called going *tropo*? Stay too long in the bush and no one wants to go home again? That was the warning given me during orientation week. *Seductive;* that was the word used. Whatever it was, I was smitten.

A gentle touch on my shoulder, and I knew I had dozed. Lena smiled down on me and motioned towards a new mug of tea beside me. I sipped the sweet lemon leaf tea and looked at the three black people in tattered *sulus* sitting with me, an oddity in their land, all of us sitting cross-legged, holding chipped mugs, pondering the endless tranquil jungle scenery. Something assenting, approving, wise, and possibly loving was very much at work here, and I gratefully let it envelop me.

We sat not speaking, not looking at one another, lazily gazing down on the grazing cattle near the stream or toward the darkening hills. The sun was low, I knew I must be on my way, but I didn't want to leave. In slow motion I pulled on my mud-covered boots, and then I said, "*Vanaka vaka levu; sa mothe,* see you next month."

One farm report down and only twenty more to go. Two miles home, a stand-up one-bucket bath and supper before the attack of the blood-sucking *manu,* the mosquito.

I hung my Coleman lamp on a nail next to my bed, climbed in, and tucked the mosquito net under my mattress. The mystery novel didn't hold my interest. A night in the hills in Fiji, the weather good, is without any earthly sound. I wanted to hear those affectionate mated parrots calling to each other. This was a night with nothing stirring, no sound other than the hum of my lamp. I could easily do without radio, television, and the dissonance that nightly news analysis brought into my life. Doing without my family, that was going to be my burden. Maybe in a couple of weeks I could travel to Suva for an overnight, find a post office, and make a telephone call to the other side of my world.

In the meantime, Beni was my immediate burden. I needed to talk to him. And soon. My farm reports meant little without the information only he could give me. I knew he lived in government housing close to the local agricultural HQ. I would rout him out.

Suni, my immediate superior and local agricultural officer, worked out of a two-room concrete-block office with no electricity. I sent a letter to Suni via Ili to give to her teacher. Suni was to ask Beni to meet me in his office. I wrote: "We are both livestock officers on this cattle farm, we are colleagues, we must work together."

Two days later I walked about one and a half hours out of the bush and caught a bus on the main road that took me into a small town and to Suni's office.

My introduction to Beni lasted all of five seconds when he and I collided in the doorway of the station office. He was running out as I walked in through a doorway too narrow to accommodate me, my knapsack, and Beni. I'm five foot seven, and Beni was a lot shorter. In our sudden body contact his face was pushed into my shoulder as he turned sideways to run past me. At that moment one of the office staffers called out, "Miss Barbara, meet your cattle scheme co-worker, Livestock Officer Beni!"

By the time this message was completed, Beni was climbing in his government Jeep, waving a careless "farewell" in my direction, spinning his wheels in the dirt road, and disappearing in a cloud of dust.

Instant impression? A red large-visored cap worn low over a young narrow black face partly hidden by oversized sunglasses, small build, underweight, childlike smirk frozen in place, frenetic energy. And the only Fijian I ever met who did not offer his hand in welcome with an emphatic, "Bula, bula." Also, the moment our bodies touched in the doorway, I smelled a strong fragrance of after-shave lotion with a distinct fruity scent. Unusual for a cattleperson to wear any scent other than a heavy dose of insecticide. Fragrances attract disease-carrying insects. In the tropics only city folk wear perfumes and scents.

At the time Beni's hasty departure was an annoyance. I resented losing half a day coming out of the bush but told myself he might have a calf in breech position or be giving a shot of penicillin to a sick cow; there could be any number of problems among 500 cows in the tropics. He was obviously a very busy man, which of course was why he needed a partner to help manage this cattle operation.

Suni didn't show surprise at Beni's hasty departure or voice any apology. Built like a chunky tree trunk, with no space between his ponderous head and his shoulders, Suni was a truly black Fijian and he wore heavy steel-rimmed glasses. He rocked in his squeaky swivel chair, behind what appeared to be a rusting World War II military-issue desk.

"Suni, I'm finding more cows than earlier reports indicate. Do you know why?"

"Have you finished all your site visits?"

"Not yet."

"These cattle wander from farm to farm. You've seen the shape of fences, sometimes no more than one strand of wire."

He definitely had a point here. Without ear tags I could be counting the same cow several times. Tagging costs money and time and there are no headgates and corrals. We spoke a few minutes, but he was anxious to get back to his paperwork. He had no comment to make when I asked him to send Beni up to my home at his earliest convenience. Suni's ambivalence said it all: *I do my job; now do yours*. This man was a bureaucrat. While we spoke he initialed typed reports without reading them. I wondered if he eventually would do the same to mine, reports that would take me hours to fill out after miles of walking hills and valleys created by ancient volcanoes.

I made up for the disappointing trek into town by finding a little restaurant that boasted three tables. After ordering a late breakfast of fried eggs and toast, I ruminated about why college-educated Suni was as uncommunicative as the farmers deep in the bush, who had no education past the sixth grade. Could it possibly be in the genes? The idea made me feel uneasy.

3
Where in Tarnation Is Beni?

In one month all the farms had been visited and reported on, and the information I had gathered was not sanguine. One fact was the most disturbing: all together the twenty-one farmers owned almost one hundred more cows and calves than bank records indicated. Where did they all come from? Data gave the annual income of these men in the vicinity of eighty dollars. Where did all that money come from to buy cattle? If the men had spare change in any amount, the money should have been sent to the Suva bank to pay off their loans.

The high head count was dangerous as well. There simply wasn't enough pasture to feed them all, and most farms didn't have grasses with good nutritional value. A lot of cows were foraging in the bush for whatever vines and leaves they could find. Eventually that would be grazed out, too.

Disease was another major worry. Not all farms showed wormy, emaciated cows, but there were far too many grade-three animals on the scheme. These must be sent to the abattoir. TB and Brucellosis testing had to begin as soon as possible. The calving rate was so low I was suspicious of spontaneous abortion due to Brucellosis. I saw no dairy cows on any of the farms, but there was no assurance that farmers were not milking some of the cows and drinking contaminated milk. Brucellosis in humans is a serious chronic disease.

Was the calving rate so low due to an acute shortage of bulls on the scheme? Did this culture believe in parthogenesis, maybe immaculate conception?

In this protein-starved country I expected to find fewer cattle. Wedding feasts, special rites of passage, and feasts celebrating returning peacekeeping soldiers sent to Lebanon were among many reasons for sacrificing an animal. And how about being just plain hungry? One evening a smiling Ili brought me a plate with five small cubes of cooked meat. Her brothers had killed a wild pig with their long wooden spears, and this was a great treat to share with me. If they didn't have the resident reporting *bulamacow* lady up the path from them, might they have been tempted to sacrifice a cow for the rare dinner of meat to break their vegetarian diet? Three times a day my neighbors ate a tasteless diet of starchy *dalo*, cassava, breadfruit, and occasionally those tiny scrolls of fernlike plants that grew wild in the bush.

Families on the scheme were obviously not eating their cattle but were accumulating more and wearing out their pastures. I had no clue as to how they were paying for these one hundred excess cattle and, more important, from whom they were buying the cattle. With proper management the farmers might raise and fatten cattle for the beef market in Fiji, but adding to the herd could bring disease to the land and also ruin pastures. I needed Beni to help me, and soon.

Answering the five "W" questions learned in Journalism 101, if applied to my co-worker Beni, always came up zero. *Who* was he? He had for several years been a civil servant, the designated livestock officer for 500 cattle on this 3,000-acre cattle operation funded by a Suva bank, which in turn had been granted the money by the World Bank. He should have been working closely with me, but I had never seen him on the farms.

Where was he? *Where* did he spend his days? He was conspicuous by his absence. Maria and Tomaci responded to my question with silence. Again they indulged in their cultural trait of gazing off to a hill on the horizon.

Why was Beni, given this job in the first place? One of the farmers said Beni had attended the University of the South Pacific and majored in agriculture. It sounded more like a two-year program, not a fully matriculating college education.

When would he see fit to meet with me and *why* was he avoiding me?

What the hell was I going to do about this ridiculous situation? I was getting physically weary and worn down walking many hours each day up and down this volcanic island of hills with only tiny flat valleys in between.

Time to face Suni. My local boss was also Beni's boss. Tomorrow I would walk out of the bush, get on the bus, go to Suni's office, and confront him. He and Beni would have to countersign my reports and mail them to the next level of management in the regional HQ in Suva.

* * *

Suni was a middle-aged man of medium height, his large, round head sitting on broad shoulders with almost no neck. He had the capacity to sit unmoving behind his desk, sinking into his body, for a long period of time. He was too well educated for this low-level job in a town hacked out of the bush and jungle. A framed yellowing parchment diploma on his office wall proved he had graduated from an Australian university and holding a bachelor's degree in agricultural engineering. He should have been working out of HQ in Suva. One more puzzlement to ponder.

I slid my backpack off my shoulders, pulled out twenty-one farm reports, looked around for a chair, and found none. Suni was obviously not going to find me one, either.

"Suni, here are all the reports on your farms. We can discuss problems I have found, or we can wait to do this when Beni is present."

With indifference Suni briefly glanced in my direction and said, "I can look at them now, initial them, and you can leave them on his desk in the front room."

"Beni and I still haven't worked together or met together. I'm not even sure I would recognize him if we passed each other on a busy street, and frankly, I'm not comfortable working on what was his job for several years. I really need to talk to him, confer with him."

Suni's eyes were on a paper on his desk when he said, "When he comes in I'll do what I can. Let me see your reports."

I always honored the cultural rules of the Fijian man living in the village not to make eye contact with me. But Suni was university-educated. He had lived at least four years in an academic, white culture. I resented his coldness in not making eye contact with me. Nevertheless, I continued to face him.

He glanced at a few of my pages but never examined them. One by one he initialed them, and when he finished he handed them back to me and asked me to place them on a vacant desk in the front room.

"Beni will read them and initial them, and the clerk will mail them out to HQ. Anything else, Barbara?"

"Well, yes, there is. Do you have someone who works out of your office who can TB-test and draw blood for Brucellosis testing?"

"TB, yes, but no blood specimens. We don't have the capacity to store blood."

"Well, then, at any rate, let's do the TB testing as soon as possible."

"Anything else?"

"The head count on this scheme. It's much higher than I was given to understand. I know that exact numbers don't mean that much, but I found almost twenty percent more cattle than I was expecting to find. Anything you can tell me would be appreciated."

Suni didn't answer right away. Then he peered out a window behind me while he spoke. "Interesting. We'll have to wait, won't we, until Beni comes in. Anything else?"

My second conference with my local boss was concluded in a few unsatisfactory minutes. I dropped my reports on a desk in the front office and looked around the hot and poorly ventilated concrete-block room. As there was no electricity, the room's only light came from two small windows and the open door. Two young Indian men smiled up at me from their desks. They obviously wanted to chat with me, but I was in no mood for pleasantries. It was immediately apparent, however, that Indian men looked directly into my eyes, and no, there was no message of aggression.

This bleak and dusty town was exactly one block long. I peered into shops so small, three customers became a crowd. Most stores sold a variety of items. In one shop I found bottles of codeine, for which one did not need a prescription, and near a window a seamstress was working on a dress for a waiting customer.

Purchases I desperately needed were meat and eggs, hopefully not spoiled. There was no electricity in this town, but the shop selling frozen meat had its own diesel generator. The owner was a hardworking young Chinese man. When he saw me looking over his cans of vegetables he joined me and asked if he could help. When he told me I could pay by check that was good news. I didn't like carrying more than a few Fijian dollars in my backpack.

"Have you met Beni's wife, Miss Barbara? She's over there by the meat counter."

"She's very pretty, isn't she? And so young. Do they live close by?"

"In government housing, close to Suni's agricultural station. Beni lives next door to Suni and his mother."

I hesitated to introduce myself to Beni's wife. I saw her furtively glance at me and then quickly turn back to the meat display. She looked ill at ease to me. A beautiful petite girl, she was slender and neat, in an attractive new-looking *sulu* and blouse. Her large eyes were bright and eager, but to judge by the quick glance she gave me, the girl was definitely feeling stressed. I wondered why.

I looked around the shop for food items not too heavy to carry back up into the hills, and when I turned back to the meat counter she was gone. I think she left without buying anything.

I wrote out my check for my provisions, and the shop owner asked, "Miss Barbara, would you like to see a chain saw I have for sale? One of your farmers might want to buy one to clear his farm for cattle grazing."

"You sell chain saws in your grocery store?"

"It's not a new chain saw, but in very good shape."

"You probably got it in barter, right? Maybe in exchange for a few months of food?"

"Beni brought it in for me to sell for him on commission. He got it from one of the local farmers."

Why did my colleague have a used chain saw he had obtained from a local farmer to give to the Chinese grocery store owner to sell on commission to another local farmer? I decided it was best to pack my food in my backpack and head off to my little home in the hills. This was something to ponder during the long trek, along with another bit of frustrating news. Why did Suni make no effort to bring his two livestock officers together in his office? Living next door to each other, the two men must meet just about every day. Yes indeed, I had good reason for a high level of frustration and puzzlement as a new uneasiness edged with anxiety took hold in me. Was Suni intentionally keeping his two livestock officers from meeting, from working together? Was it time to confer with a higher level in the Fijian bureaucracy, and if I did, how many enemies would then emerge on my local level?

One hundred head of cattle, some young calves, were each worth between $100.00 and $175.00. With the average yearly income of Fijian farmers around $80 where did all this money come? High time for a visit to regional HQ in Suva.

4
Bats in the Vale Lailai

My skin is black. Not as black as that of Chief Siti, but not as light as that of someone with one white and one black parent. The sin of vanity intact, I remain a redhead, however, with a crown of tight, frizzy Fijian curls. I walk the bush paths barefoot wearing a bright red *sulu* tied high on my chest but wearing no shirt and no bra. That is a vitally important detail. My neighbor in the bush Maria, mother of seven children, frequently went about her chores bare-breasted, with her *sulu* tied only around her waist. After the birth of one child, women are permitted to do this in their home and in their village. In my dream my breasts, thank goodness, are covered, another adaptation and compromise.

After this very pleasant and completely proper dream I knew it was now safe to travel to Suva. Returning home from a big-city environment to my humble *bure* was now a certainty: I was coping well and felt close to my new culture. This balancing act of going a little *tropo* without going over the edge and, heaven forbid, actually running around in the bush bare-breasted, even in a dream, was an immensely important step.

This was the reason I did not leave the bush for several months. My bosses did not set rules for my coming to Suva. It was my choice to stay in the silence of the bush for as long as it took me to get used to being the only white woman within more miles than I cared to know.

During the first month I was afflicted with symptoms of withdrawal, daily annoyances coping with no running water, electricity, stove, refrigeration, or telephone. With no transportation for milk, bread, and groceries, I carried all my food in my knapsack, usually shopping on Saturdays. I had to go cold turkey from a lifetime of high-tech comfort and coddling, which had abruptly come to a halt. My reward every night after these early uncomfortable days was reading in bed under mosquito netting by the light of a Coleman lamp. The enfolding white shroud "wedding" veil softly blurred my surrounding bamboo walls. The mosquitoes settling outside the net by the hundreds, I teased them by placing my finger on the inside and moving them as if with a magnet. In my sleep if I didn't stay centered on my mat I'd wake to sucking mosquitoes on any part of my body touching the netting. Bone-breaking dengue fever was always a clear and present danger.

After I awoke from my wonderful dream, I knew I had made a smooth transition into a Fijian, a redheaded one. I knew it was now safe to visit the big Fijian "apple" called Suva.

* * *

I walked the several miles down the path to the main road and waited for the bus to the capital. A bus came that would take me to my local boss, Suni. I was again tempted to confront him about the absent Beni. Who was paying Beni's salary? Was it the World Bank grant or Fijian Ministry of Agriculture money? If it was the World Bank, I had muscle. Without this fact I jeopardized relationships locally and also in Suva HQ. Questioning the Brits in Suva was a smarter move. Behavior modification, conflict avoidance, this was what village life had taught me. There are no alpha types in the bush to raise stress levels. Even the chief bent to the wishes of a large body of elders. The problems on the cattle scheme couldn't be solved on the local level. I had to go to the next level of bureaucracy given only to white men, and that was in Suva.

The capital was in flux; the grandest and most luxurious British colonial governor's mansion in the Pacific shared a lawn with a Howard Johnson Hotel. A Fijian policeman walked his beat, tall and proud, wearing a white pith helmet, white shirt, and white *sulu* skirt, hem cut with long points flapping around his knees, and holding a billy club. As in England, the police carry no guns here.

Some blocks away from the hotels, close to the busy harbor, is a crowded and clamorous city market. Mostly the women worked their booths with tables piled high with *dalo,* bananas, papaw, eggplant, and every other vegetable and fruit grown on the island. I recognized Chief Siti's wife, Zeta, standing behind a mound of shiny deep purple eggplants. Unlike her silent, composed self in the village, Zeta was in a joyful animated conversation with her neighbors. These women left their villages in the dark early hours taking to market vegetables they grew in their *tei tei,* their gardens.

Also close to the harbor is a rank and acrid-smelling pierside bar. A drunken aggregate of Russian, Australian, French, American, and Fijian sailors on liberty from their freighters shouted at one another. A sweating three-hundred-pound off-duty policeman leaned against the front door jamb fanning himself, bored and waiting for the next brawl.

I was soon unnerved by the constant boisterous noise of Suva. An uneasy creeping panic took hold. The murmuring whispers of the distant bush had been within a day replaced by the incessant discordant noise of traffic. Rudely shoved and jostled by strangers of many races, I was dizzy with the dissonance. My eyes burned, my head ached from diesel fumes, and I hurriedly searched for a quiet place—anyplace would do—and finally took refuge in a pizza shop. I found a table in the rear corner away from the cacophony of the throng of people outside. Why this anxiety? I vowed to come out of the bush more often. Being overwhelmed by the noises of a minuscule third world city into this wretched state would never do. Never in the years of working in New York, a city of seven million, traveling in packed subways, had I felt the apprehension I felt on this day. I would have to come out of the bush more often, at least once a month, maybe more.

Regional HQ Veterinary Officer Richard was a tall, aristocratic-looking young blond man born and raised in London. He stood behind his desk, shook my hand, and came sternly to the point, asking, "Barbara, have you been sick? Months on the job and we haven't received one single farm report from your scheme."

"I don't understand. All the farms have been visited, and the reports were all put on Beni's desk in my local station office for Beni and Suni to initial. Suni said this was the procedure; Beni would mail them to you."

Richard studied his desk blotter and frowned. He finally sat down and informed me, "He did not forward them to this office. That is the procedure, Barbara. We should see one report for each farm each month. I look them over, initial them, and relay them and other paperwork to the loan officer at the bank."

I stared at him not knowing how to integrate this bad news, how to respond to him, when I felt like the dunce of the year. Were both Suni and Beni blindsiding me? Or only

Beni? Whoever it was, he was responsible for Richard losing respect for me.

"It's important to me not to break protocol. I always assumed Beni or Suni would send my paperwork on to you."

"You may easily assume too much, Barbara. This isn't Britain, and it's not the USA." He directed his slow, wry smile at his desk blotter. While he spoke he slowly made a triangle out of his pen, pencil, and ruler. "From now on mail your reports directly to me. Mail them from the post office next to Suni's office. Don't take them into the office at all. Break the established pattern; it isn't working now and hasn't been working in the past."

Was Richard telling me there had been problems before I came? Was this his way of saying, "Cut to the chase; stop all that nonsense on the scheme, and let's get going with what has to be done up there in the hills?"

Instead of saying this, he asked,

"Have you been working with Beni? That was the original plan."

"Not yet. We passed each other in the doorway of the station when I first arrived. He ran out so fast I'm not sure I would even recognize him if we passed each other on the street or, for that matter, on the bush path."

"He hasn't been seen on the cattle scheme since you arrived? Interesting. Would you like a cup of tea?"

"Yes, I would. Richard, do you have any suggestions for me? I don't know if I can keep it up, covering three thousand acres every month. It's a devil of a lot of walking. I need Beni to take some of the workload."

Richard's eyes focused on an ant zigzagging across his blotter. He seemed fascinated by the ant.

Still watching the ant, Richard said, "Let me read your reports first before I know what to advise. You should have brought them with you. Next time you come into town come to see me again, Good; here is our tea."

The Indian office boy brought two cups of hot tea, and when the office door closed I expected Richard and I could discuss the absent Beni. Instead, Richard smiled at me and quickly asked, "Did your village initiate you with the bats in the *vale lailai* ceremony?"

I shook my head no. Clearly he was signaling that the topic of Beni was now history. Getting information out of Richard was not going well.

He laughed loudly and said, "Well, that in itself says something about how the village folk perceive you. They must respect you or need your help enough to have saved you the embarrassment of your life."

"The welcoming ceremony was an embarrassment; I didn't need another one. What about the bats in the outhouse ceremony?"

"Last year a young woman teacher came from England to a village on one of the other islands, and she didn't survive her first initiation."

"She died?"

"Nothing so harsh, although for a few minutes she thought she was in a hellish fix. When she got to her *bure* she needed to use her brand-new *vale lailai*. In less than a minute she ran out screaming, her slacks around her ankles. She ran into her *bure* and packed her things. Within forty-eight hours she was back in England."

"No plumbing and she went clear out of her mind—was that it?"

"Not exactly. The new outhouse had been built several months before the teacher came, and no one had used it. It was the most primitive outhouse, with just a hole in the ground. Bats had taken possession of the new underground cave, hundreds, maybe thousands of them. And when she used the new *vale lailai* they came up between her—"

It didn't take a wildly creative imagination to feel sympathy for the young teacher, but Richard's laughter was contagious and it felt wonderful to laugh with a man, a white man with whom I could safely make eye contact.

I was so relaxed and at ease after the story that I almost left HQ without asking Richard about Beni's salary. If it was World Bank money, I was in a position to get him back to work. If the Fijian Ministry of Agriculture paid his salary, I was in trouble. I had reason to believe that Suni, for whatever reason, wasn't in charge of his own office. Beni was running amok, and I had lost hope that Suni would discipline him.

Richard stood up and extended his hand in a farewell gesture. I backed away and said, "Richard, I can't go back to the cattle scheme without some answers. Who pays Beni his salary? Where does he spend his workdays? Where are all those excess cattle coming from?"

In Richard's defense, I knew he had attempted to answer me, but I could not read his young, serious face, which showed not the least emotion. He had closed himself to me.

"His salary comes out of the Ministry of Agriculture budget. Mine and the all wages of all the other Brits are paid by other agencies. Barbara, stop by the next time you're in the city. Now I really have an appointment to keep."

He grasped my hand in farewell and guided me out of the door.

Riding home in the bus, I mused over whether even Richard hesitated to discipline Beni and, if so, why? One fact was clear: Beni's salary was Fijian money. Fijians never fire one of their own. In this country only the more serious crimes against humanity are punishable. A cow? Even allowing 100 hungry, possibly diseased cows to spread their diseases to their owners was probably not considered punishable under the law.

A friend back home who had completed a tour of duty as a public health nurse in the Congo told me a technique she used when epidemics struck and she saw little hope for her village. She always asked herself, "How does one eat an elephant? One bite at a time." On the bus ride back into the hills, I asked the question: "How does one bring order to almost 600 cattle in poor condition? One cow at a time—one cow at a time...."

5
Don't Bulls Have Rights, Too?

After the pleasant, but wasted, time I had spent with Richard in his office, I wasn't at all sure that it was possible to make changes even with his assistance. In the hierarchy of the Ministry he also had a boss, Dr. Stevens, an Irishman, who in turn answered to a Brit, Thomas Mitchell. I had never met either of these men. However, before I moved up the ladder of perceived power there was a decision that Richard had the full responsibility of making: how to bring breeding bulls to the scheme. I had the responsibility of removing grade-three and diseased cattle and calves. I decided to push a lot harder on Richard, no more "nice American lady" approach.

Two months after meeting with Richard, I walked into Suni's office and waited for him to leave his office for his lunch break, then telephoned Richard.

"Richard, I still haven't seen Beni and I can't wait any longer."

"Barbara, you're going to have to go it alone; there's nothing to be done. But I will talk to Suni again. Sorry."

"I'm sorry, too. Next week I have to move out fifty head of grade-three cows to the abattoir. Please call them and tell them to be ready and to send the trucks."

"Can do. But that is a lot of cows. You sure it's necessary?"

"These cows may not make it through the coming dry season anyway. Ideally more cows should go, but the farmers won't hear of it. Our pastures are in poor shape."

"Understood. Anything else?"

"Yes, there is. How do we go about bringing nine or ten good breeding bulls to the scheme? The 'shower of gold from above,' the immaculate conception theory, doesn't seem to be as reliable as the Bible would have us believe."

For a moment there was only silence, then, "You probably should go one level higher than my office. That's Stevens; he will have to approve that large an outlay of money."

"Of course, but you will have to approve my request. I'm here, and you're there. Please talk to him."

"And somebody will have to travel up north where the Ministry's breeding farms are and look the bulls over."

"All you need is a Jeep; you, Beni, Stevens, you can all do it. I don't have transportation."

Richard's voice took on an angry edge. "Not bloody likely I'd send Beni. Barbara, why not wait a year, let the grasses recover during the rainy season?"

I hesitated a moment. It occurred to me that every time I spoke to Richard I was giving him bad news. It was impossible to be diplomatic in my line of work.

I took a deep breath and said, "Richard, I may not be here in one year. For the sake of the cattle scheme it's best to do it now. I aim to move out more grade-three cows as soon as I can."

After a long silence, he replied, "We'll see. Get back to you. Don't hold your breath, Barbara," and the phone went dead.

A month later the jungle vine wireless service sent me a message telling me to show up at Richard's office to look over twenty-five bulls that had been transported into town. For me the news was Christmas in Fiji.

*   *   *

Richard drove me to the livestock holding corrals where shipments of breeding stock were held for examination, testing, and sales. We sat on top of a wood-fenced corral and looked down on one of the most pitiful scenes I have ever seen in my whole life of cattle breeding; twenty-five bulls, blood trickling down their faces, terrified, huddled motionless in the far corner. These animals were under the worst kind of stress. The searing afternoon sun beat down on them, and I saw no water or feed. They were dehydrated, and their heads hung low.

The bloodlines were the best. That was the good part, a good mix for the tropics, a Brahman cross-breed, cattle that can twitch their skin to rid them of biting flies. The bulls were well built, long-legged, long-bodied. And the bad news: they had been dehorned and not by professionals. One bull showed a thin stream of blood still spurting sideways from his wound, and the rest had unnecessarily lost blood. Dehorning is not always a priority. Bulls can be shipped without injury to each other. But back in the States, serious cattle breeders in the Midwest never own horned cattle. I had no experience with dehorning, but I knew there was a right and a wrong way to do this cruel cutting.

I slid down the fence into the corral and moved closer to this frightened herd of bulls. Moving very slowly, I looked back, expecting Richard to join me. We were, after all, here to pick out bulls for the scheme. He not only hadn't moved from his place on the fence but also had a wide-eyed, alert expression on his face. Well, I decided he probably was as pained by this bloody scene as I was. Or was he afraid?

I moved only within twenty feet of the bulls. But with every step they crowded closer together, pressing against the walls of their corral. These animals were traumatized and terrified of me. Their behavior said it all. Back home I had routinely walked into my field that had as many as six yearling bulls together. They would surround me and nudge me, curious and friendly. If one got too chummy, all anyone needed to do was smack him on the soft part of his nose with a hand or a fist and he would back off. With my older herd bull I always had a strong stick to smack him on his nose. But these mistreated bulls were all in a state of shock.

I climbed back up the fence and questioned a white man who was also sitting on the fence next to Richard. He told us the bulls had been transported in diesel-fueled trucks from the north side of the island, the trip was well over twenty hours due to the mountains, and the bulls had not been given a rest or water and feed the entire trip. These animals had experienced long hours of body-to-body contact in high temperatures, breathing poisonous diesel fumes from exhaust pipes under the truck, and then immediately were dehorned as they were off-loaded. After all that insult it would be a miracle if the weaker ones survived the next few weeks.

Richard never did get off the fence. Obviously, for some reason he was afraid of these animals. He asked to have them moved around by several Fijian workers armed with sharp pointed clubs. Slowly we picked out ten bulls to be transported to the scheme. When that day came I would get the biggest surprise of my life working the cattle scheme. Beni appeared.

There was a lot of excitement when the truck arrived filled with ten bulls. All the farmers on the scheme surrounded the truck, speaking little, tensed for the frenzy of unloading excited bulls. The back gate was pushed sideways, giving only one bull enough space to escape. Three men threw lassos around the bull's head as he pushed through. Before his front hooves hit the ground the bull was struggling but under control.

I worried about how these men were going to secure their bulls on their farms to keep them from wandering off. Recently I had the sad sight of a cow dead from strangulation when a farmer had tied her to a tree. The nursing calf was attempting to suckle milk out of her dead mother. I wished fervently the men would stop this practice of roping cattle to trees. I also hoped the farmers had built corrals out of their ubiquitous bamboo groves. There was bamboo fencing material available, six inches and more in diameter, growing close to my *bure*.

The unloading and the roping went better than we all had expected. No one was hurt and the bulls soon calmed down. The men moved fast, working together, trusting one another, and no one showed anger or frustration. The comradery of these village-born men was a joy to watch—no posturing, no egos gone amok. Fijians are born team players. One by one bulls and men disappeared up the path. For some it would be several hours before they reached their farflung farms.

The Brits in their own country put rings in bulls' noses. In the Midwest we always had hefty leather halters with short chains encircling muzzles for control. Here in Fiji both practices were too pricey. Cattle management in this third world country was so much more stressful for the animals than back home, where we had stout holding pens and loading chutes. Not for the first time, I wondered if there wasn't a more efficient source of protein for the many malnourished Fijians.

When these scheme bulls arrived at the farms their necks would be covered with rope burns for flies to lay eggs on and they would need to be medicated. It would take a whole day to travel to Suva and back for any medicines. I felt a combination of relief that we finally had good breeding stock and a deep worry about the stress on these animals.

The Indian truck drivers asked me to sign documents and quickly drove away, leaving me standing alone gazing after them.

I heard a bus approaching on its way to Suni's office. Maybe I should drop off the paperwork and have a meal in the small town. Or I could head back up the path and home. A movement above me in the woods, partway up a small hill, caught my attention. A man stood up from a crouching position, pulled a red cap out of his back pocket, and put it on. He came down from his perch, agile and graceful as a cat, his movements slow and bouncing, even languid. Before he approached me he stopped and looked up the road. Was he waiting for his ride or a bus?

"Miss Barbara! Those were good bulls."

"And you are?"

"You don't remember me? I'm Beni."

We shook hands, or rather he reached for mine before I could pull back. His hand felt delicate-boned, childlike. He wore a strong-smelling after-shave lotion with a pungent fruity aroma. On his wrist he wore a gold watch with a broad gold band. This was no twenty-five-dollar Timex but flashy and costly. Now that he was here, finally within sight of the cattle scheme, I wasn't at all sure I gave a damn. I was surprised, yes, but not caring. For weeks now I had known that somehow, someway, I must do my job without his help. And why hadn't he make his whereabouts known to me and all the farmers before the bulls were unloaded?

Had the farmers seen him crouching up in the woods? They must have. Nothing escapes the Fijian living in the bush. They all pretended they didn't see him? Why? Maybe on this day, excited about their new bulls, the men were too engrossed and didn't know their livestock officer was watching them from behind the trees. A child could figure out that this was a man who enjoyed watching people in secret and could be very patient while doing so.

Beni was a small-boned man, with the slim body of a teenager, and wore tight new blue jeans and a black shirt with a tiny alligator on the pocket. He wore his large visored red cap pulled low over his face and never took off his oversize mirrored sunglasses. His permanent broad grin showed glistening white teeth in a completely black face. Not a drop of alien blood in this man's genetic pool. His features, what I could see of them, were close to being feminine: a small pointed chin and a narrow ridged nose with delicately flaring nostrils. His face was set in a determined grin. He glanced toward the main road. His body language told me he wasn't going to hang around in conversation any longer than he chose to.

I plunged ahead. "Beni, why do the farmers have more cows than the bank reports indicate the farmers bought with their loan money?"

Before he answered, he again glanced up the road. He obviously was waiting to catch a ride or a bus.

"If they do, you should be asking the farmers. They are not schoolchildren. You are not their teacher to scold them. If they get more cattle, that is their way of running their farms."

"There isn't enough forage. Some of these cows are starving."

"*Senga na lenga,* no problem; we have a ratio of five acres to each cow."

"Wrong, Beni, it is a problem when those five acres are mostly the wrong grasses or covered with bush and trees. In this scheme we should never exceed one cow for every ten acres."

Beni's childlike grin finally faded. "Barbara, you know nothing about my land, my country. You know less than the farmers about cattle. Go back to your America and leave this cattle scheme to us."

Again he glanced toward the bus route. I had too little time. He was going to elude me once more. My anger got the best of me. I used the only weapon I had to work with.

"Beni, I sent at least fifty emaciated grade-three cows to the abattoir, and soon I will send more."

He jammed his red cap even lower over his face. His lithe body stiffened into a combat-ready fighting posture. His chin jutted out as he shook a finger at me and yelled, "You don't have the right to make that decision! You don't. Leave all those cattle exactly where they are."

"You leave me no choice. To bring so many cattle on this land will destroy it. In a few years you will make a desert out of your land."

Beni moved closer to me and pointed a finger from each hand at my face. "Barbara, go home. If you send more of these cattle away, it will be the last decision you make."

For a moment we stood face to face, and it was much too close for me. I used all the fortitude I had not to step back. Beni continued to face me. In his anger he was panting. I smelled tobacco and, to my surprise, alcohol. This man must be out of control to drink whiskey in this noonday heat.

Beni was considering saying more when we both heard the noise of the diesel-fueled bus approaching. He threw up his hands and made an unpleasant animal-like grunting sound. He turned, ran toward the bus, and like a trained stunt man leaped on board as it was moving away. It was the bus that traveled in the direction of Suva.

    A fierce and strange man, this Beni. After many months of his absence, he showed up to view the unloading of expensive bulls and didn't hang around long enough to greet farmers he has known for years but watched from behind trees. He had a poor grasp, or gave the impression of ignorance, of how to maintain the health and condition of a herd. And he became instantly hostile at my decision to send grade-three cows to market.

    But one fact he knew from the very beginning of my arrival on the scheme: he knew the two of us could never work together. That's why he never showed his face. It wasn't that I was a woman; a Fijian woman would have been no problem in his culture. He would dominate her. But I was a white woman.

    The old British colonial culture, even after ten years of Fijian independence, was ingrained in Beni's cognition: he had been born under colonial rule. His tirade was proof of his bitterness in losing control of his cattle scheme and his unbridled hate for the white woman responsible. His fury had been growing within him for months. On that day he threatened me. He was too clever to tell me how he would retaliate. And why his violent reaction? They weren't his cows—or were they? Whenever the farmers were questioned as to where all the extra cows and calves came from, their gaze wandered listlessly into the jungle. The answer to that question hit me hard. As many as 20 percent of the entire herd belonged to Beni. And that was why he was hiding in the woods. His curiosity got the best of him. He needed to see the bulls who would father his calves. There was no doubt that Suni knew of Beni's deception. Why didn't he fire the guy? Richard probably also knew and for some reason chose to ignore the problem.

I felt humiliated, angry, and powerless. To save the herd grade-three cows had to be sacrificed, and yet Beni was going to wreak havoc because some of these belonged to him.

I had no appetite for that meal in town now. It was too hot to sit on the bench and wait for a bus that might or might not come. I trudged back up the path to my *bure*. Three questions nagged at me: Where did Beni spend his days? If Beni was going to retaliate, how and where?

6
Who's in Charge Anyway?

Tom Mitchell, in his bored nasal British voice, announced the transport of twenty-five breeding bulls into the region's cattle station. I ran my fingers through my hair and made an effort to look interested. This was old and unpleasant business for me but it was time to pay attention. Those were my bulls he was talking about, and maybe that was why I was summoned to this dreary meeting.

Mitchell slipped a new tape into his tape recorder and asked, "Barbara, may we assume the bulls made it safely to your cattle scheme?"

The eyes of a dozen agricultural staffers, half Indian and half Fijian, settled on me. My chair squeaked as I slid closer to the conference table. Did Mitchell want me to stick to the facts of the bull transport or did he want a sanitized, "Yes indeed, they arrived safely"? Mitchell saw my hesitation and nodded at me to begin. A sudden movement of Suni, who had been dozing in his chair beside me, told me he was awake. He took off his sunglasses when I glanced at him, and I saw an expression I had seen only once before, when I had questioned his bookkeeping methods. He was warning me to tread lightly. I glanced at Richard and saw that he was fascinated with his fingernails. Early signs of jungle rot, maybe? I had about one and a half years to go on my contract with the Ministry. I had no intention of letting my cattle scheme go belly up. Still fuming over the cruel treatment of my bulls, I charged ahead, sticking to the facts.

Facing Mitchell, my voice flat and casual, I answered, "The bulls showed obvious symptoms of stress. The dehorning process needs to be upgraded. There was unnecessary loss of condition in these bulls. The drivers of the transport trucks took turns driving well over twenty hours without watering the bulls and giving them a rest in a fenced field. During transport, depending on the weather and the crowding, cattle can lose close to fifteen percent of their body weight over the first few hours. Every hour beyond that adds to their stress, and they lose more weight. This transport was unnecessarily harsh. Two of the bulls, now on the cattle scheme, are sick and unable to service the cows. Several more are in poor shape. They wander away from their herds and isolate themselves, which is not normal behavior."

In the silence that followed my report I clearly felt the floor move under me. Was it a heavy diesel truck passing outside or was I feeling the jarring dissonance of angry staff members staring at me from around the table? My mouth was dry after giving my report, so I got up, poured myself a glass of warm water, and took my time drinking it before returning to my seat. By that time all eyes were again focused on Mitchell.

He slowly and methodically slid the used tape out of the recorder, made a notation on it, and put a new tape back in. He picked up his agenda notes, languidly turned a few pages, and requested one of the Indians to report on the latest cocoa harvest.

I looked at Richard and saw that he wore a benign but satisfied expression while writing in his notebook. Mitchell's meeting droned on another hour, but Richard's eyes never met mine. Suni sat bolt upright, very much awake. He spent the rest of the meeting lighting cigarettes from the glowing stubs of previous ones.

For several months I had successfully avoided my top boss, the Englishman Thomas Mitchell. Civil servants warned me that the monthly meetings he chaired in Suva moved at the speed of a sleepy slug, and you should wear your sunglasses so he won't see you snooze off. Mitchell, a diplomatic Brit educated in the same school as Queen Elizabeth's sons, was categorized as a supremely able "company man."

Mitchell understood there was always an ambitious well-educated Indian lurking close by who had designs on his job and would waste no time in replacing Fijians with Indians in Ministry jobs. Mitchell also knew that if he himself was replaced by a Fijian, many skilled Indians would be let go to favor a Fijian majority with a questionable education.

Mitchell had a reputation for working ten hours a day and doing something no administrator had ever done before: he communicated equally with the Indians and the Fijians and kept the peace. In his long, solemn, meetings he was a nonreactor. He kept the Indians and Fijians docile and polite to each other in the politically charged atmosphere of this newly independent nation.

Suni asked me to attend Mitchell's monthly meetings. I complained that an entire day traveling by bus was nonsense. He said he would drive me, and I relented. A Jeep without shock absorbers was a luxury compared to a dusty open-air bus spitting diesel fuel. It wasn't until days after the tedious afternoon meeting that I decided Richard had ordered Suni to bring me.

Mitchell looked decidedly British Colonial Empire in his white starched short-sleeve shirt, knee-length navy blue shorts, and knee-high navy blue stockings. With carefully groomed sleek dark hair, good-looking, suntanned, maybe a yachtsman, he was stocky and looked fit. During the long meeting his expression never wavered from one of grave affability and serenity.

When I sat down at the large conference table I recognized only Veterinary Officer Richard. The Indians and Fijians were strangers to me. I was surprised that Mitchell had no secretary taking notes. He either had no one capable of shorthand or needed to edit and clean up every word spoken. As he was a good company man, the latter might have been the reason.

Suni drove us out of Suva, and before leaving the town of Nausori for the long drive into the hills he stopped at a store and bought two one-liter bottles of Fiji Bitters Beer. He had not said a word since we left HQ, which was not too unusual. Like most Fijian men, he was the silent type. But not this silent. Any attempt on my part to begin a conversation failed dismally. He hunched over the wheel, concentrating on the road.

We began the gentle climb into the hills, where drivers needed to avoid large rolling rocks and holes in the rough dirt road. Suni's strong masculine profile, with a high slanting forehead over deep-set eyes, showed his usual composed self. With his education, why was he stuck in the bush in a small cinder-block building without electricity and plumbing, with only his mother keeping house for him? He was clearly Suva HQ material. I had seen an electric refrigerator in his kitchen, which his mother used as a closet. At one time he must have lived in Suva.

"Barbara, open one of the beers for me."

I offered him an open bottle, and he told me to take a swallow first. Even warm beer can flush down road dust, and I took several swallows. I handed him the bottle and watched as he held it in one hand, drove the Jeep with the other, and when he came to a straight patch of road up-ended the bottle and drink half of it without taking it from his lips.

"Just what the doctor ordered. Open up the other bottle, Barbara. We're only halfway home, and the dust gets thicker the higher we climb."

"Sounds good to me, Suni. After a dumb meeting that didn't need either one of us to be there, Fiji Bitters Beer may yet save the day."

I waited for a response, any response. I wanted a reaction from Suni. Though I was embarrassed to admit it, I needed his support on the cattle scheme. More silence. Suni turned on the headlights. In the hills the change from day into night comes too quickly for dusk to have its time.

He upended the nearly empty bottle and drained it in one long swallow and tossed it out the window.

"Barbara, you made four very serious enemies today. You will have to face consequences."

"What I did today was attempt to improve the transport of cattle in temperatures over one hundred degrees."

"All three Indian drivers of those trucks transporting the twenty-five bulls were sitting at the table today."

"Suni, what I saw was cruelty to domestic animals."

"You are not in the USA; you're in Fiji. Face it; you're not going to change the Indian."

"I have to try. We are talking worst-case transport conditions."

"Indians don't eat beef. Indians eat only goat. They have no feeling for cattle. Sometimes I think they have no feeling for anything but their wallets."

"Suni, I must try. That's why I'm here."

Without emotion he said, "Keep doing what you're doing and you may not get out of this country alive."

"Suni, you're not going to frighten me that easily."

"You also made an enemy of the Fijian who dehorned those bulls. He was sitting next to me. He was very angry."

"If that is what it takes, Suni, if that is what it takes."

"Barbara, your report made your observations abundantly clear. Now you will face abundant consequences."

"The farmers deserve better. I've seen the bulls who are now on the farms. Too many of them are not happy campers."

"You criticized men in front of their superior, the British Minister of Agriculture, Mitchell."

"So they lost face?"

"Yes indeed; they will never forget what you did."

"Saving face takes precedence over cruelty to animals."

Suni's silence affirmed my words. In the darkness I couldn't read him; I only knew that the silence was an unfriendly one. But maybe he was only concentrating on his driving.

"I'm thirsty as hell, Barbara; you drink first."

This bumpy road into the hills was a road to hell. I never could drink neatly out of a bottle and soon my shirt smelled like a brewery, but the beer was definitely helping to modify my cranky responses to Suni. I was beginning to feel downright chipper.

I offered him the fresh bottle, and he took a long drink and handed it back to me.

"I suppose next time I see something wrong I should talk to the guilty party directly and in private."

"Maybe and maybe not."

"Suni, I can't read you. I don't know what you mean."

"I don't know what you considered wrong."

He did not know what I considered wrong. We were culturally so far distant from each other that this agriculturalist did not see wrongful treatment of expensive breeding stock. With Suni, maybe what he did not say was as important as what he did say.

After a long silence, he replied, "Barbara, in Fiji we moved through our days making only little ripples. You come to us and you make waves. Today you made a tsunami. One thing you must remember: do not make an enemy of Beni, never. Remember that."

"Ay, yes, Beni, my counterpart. The absent Fijian livestock officer. We bumped into each other once again when the bulls were unloaded."

"You have seen him only that one time on the scheme?

"That's right."

"He has never helped you on the farms?"

"No."

"Ha! Soon, he will come again. Very soon now. Yes indeed."

Suni handed me the bottle of beer, and this time I refused more shirt-drenching sips. I still had a long trek up a path in the night without a moon. Maybe my flashlight was in my backpack and maybe not. Nevertheless, I was feeling quite carefree and pleasant.

"Suni, if it takes a tsunami for those Indians to take heed of the bulls' needs, then that's what I'm here for."

7
Liku

My pillow damp with sweat sliding off my forehead smelled musty, a familiar odor in the Fijian tropics when bedding isn't hung out in the sun every day. This was my second day in bed after the crazy calf-dog-farmer accident. All three of these creatures were crazy animals. Quite possibly I was the fourth.

The accident was waiting to happen: without a corral, without proper fencing, not one cattle restraining headgate on 3,000 acres, why did I attempt to help a sick three-hundred-pound heifer calf? I was surely the crazy one. The Fijian farmer asked me to examine his well-bred calf, who had sores over most of her body. In the tropics there are skin problems no midwestern farmer would have a clue about treating. The best way was to get a skin scraping and take it to the vet's lab in Suva. Under a microscope possibly I might get a diagnosis and use the correct medication.

I never should have tried roping this calf. Every one of those 500 or more head of cattle I was under contract to manage were wildly fearful of any kind of handling. The first step was deceptively easy. I lassoed the calf and secured the other end of the rope to a post. The calf went into a gyrating panic, and I jerked her head to the ground. I wrapped the rope around the calf's front legs, then heard a crack. The rope went slack and I didn't have to look. I knew the post had snapped. I threw myself on top of the squealing calf's chest to grab the rope and get it around her back legs. Just then the farmer's wild bush dog heard the calf's squealing and attacked her belly. The farmer came running with his machete and swung at the dog's head. I heard the hiss of the machete close to my ear and the *thunk* of the knife as it laid open the dog's skull. I lost all my concentration on the calf. My hands weakened the grip on the rope. The calf stumbled up wildly, the rope still around her legs and also mine. She fought free of the rope, regained her freedom, and disappeared into the jungle, but not before trampling and twisting my foot and ankle into the ground of hard clay.

The farmer looked down at the bloodied limp body of his dog. He was embarrassed, but I saw no grief. There were too many of these semiwild bush dogs roaming the bush. He did know he should have tied up his dog before I came.

He smiled sheepishly and mumbled a few "senga na lengas." Then he asked me to follow him to his bamboo *bure* for a rest, and his wife would serve us tea.

The short walk to his home was getting more painful with each step, and my limping caught his attention. With his blood-streaked machete he cut a long pole, something I could lean on. I declined the tea. The sooner I got home, the sooner I could lie down.

Leaning on the stick, I hobbled several miles home. It felt as if every bone, tendon, and ligament in the foot and ankle was now skewed and twisted. I could only hope there was no fracture. Walking all the way down the bush path to catch a bus to the local clinic was out of the question. Time to bite the bullet.

By the second day my cattle boot wouldn't fit over my swollen and mishapen foot and ankle. But that was irrelevant, because the sharp pains kept me in bed. Just getting out of bed and taking care of basics made me dizzy and nauseous.

I reread a few chapters of Thoreau's *Walden,* which in the past usually brought balance and a healthy perspective to my world. Not on this afternoon. Before, I had always read about his concept of gratitude for felt physical pain when I was without any pain. This afternoon with my foot on fire, the corrugated tin roof of my bamboo *bure* sizzling hot, I knew I was alive. I didn't need Thoreau to remind me to count my blessings because I lay in agony; therefore, I lived. Why did this man use pain to understand his role in the world?

My eyes followed the long-tailed *moco,* miniature lizards, running along the roof beams over my head. Tweezer-shaped jaws suddenly opened, and a needle tongue flicked out, curling around an insect. *Moco* darted in and out of view through tiny openings in the woven bamboo walls, running upside down and around the beams playing tag in a frenzy of motion. I thought again of Thoreau. He had always planned his life according to his concept of deferred pleasure. And here I was being harmlessly entertained by these lowly reptiles having one helluva lot more fun in their short lives than Thoreau ever had.

In a little more than one year my contract with the Ministry of Agriculture would be null and void, but in the interim there was a lot of work to be done. Maybe next week with the help of three men working together we could get a skin scraping of the calf's eruptions and send the specimen to the city for diagnosis. In six months in the tropics I had never seen such a virulent form of skin disease. And it was a calf with good breeding—long legs, long, well-muscled body, not like the runts I usually saw. And if one calf was afflicted there would shortly be more casualties. The stress on their immune system would lead to incurable diseases.

A soft knock came on my open door, and eleven-year-old Ili stepped over the sill and put down two buckets of water.

"Miss Barbara, are you getting better?"

"I don't know, Ili; I really don't know. Tell me about what happened in school today."

"The teacher said there was an American satellite that was going to crash to Earth."

"Don't worry, Ili. Our planet is so big, and the satellite is so small. There really isn't anything to worry about."

"But Fiji is only a tiny dot on our world map. If we are hit, we will be all gone."

This wasn't the first time Ili had come home from school and reported a ridiculous story rooted in the more civilized world told by her teacher.

Ili was serious about school. She wanted to go all the way through school in the village until she was sixteen years old and then go to live with a relative in Suva and graduate from high school. None of her older sisters had gone on. Only rarely did Ili smile, only when I brought back a bit of candy for her from a daylong trip to regional HQ.

Ili was light-skinned, with delicate features. Her father was coal black, her mother looked to be a mocha brown Polynesian, and their seven children were colored in a variety of shades, all different from their parents. Did Captain Cook's sailors hundreds of years ago find time for gene pooling during their sandalwood timbering?

Ili knelt beside my bed. In her world it would be an insult to me to have her head higher than mine.

"Miss Barbara, did you kill any rats last night? All the rocks are lying against the wall."

"I aimed at three. There's a little one. Must be a new arrival. The others are bigger and older and quite bold. The one I really want to hit is the one that balances overhead on the wire, trying to get to my Velveeta cheese in the string bag. He should be in a circus."

"Miss Barbara, you should have a cat."

"Can't! Might get attached to it. Don't have any food for it."

"You can't cook for yourself. I will bring you some *dalo* after mother cooks tonight."

"Can cats eat root vegetables?"

"Our bush cats eat what we eat, just like our bush dogs."

Ili carried all the rocks to my bedside and made a little mountain out of them just as she had done many times before.

"Miss Barbara, my mother said she sent my brother to Liku's *bure* to tell her to come to you. She will treat your foot."

"She's a nurse?"

"Not a nurse like in the clinic. She knows bush medicine from her mother and her grandmother. She is my father's aunt's cousin's stepdaughter. Mother said she helped me be born."

Although it was always hard not to laugh at extended family descriptions, it was best not to comment. Almost a teenager, Ili already knew when she might make eye contact with a boy and when it was a family taboo. In these isolated, ingrown villages Ili knew exactly to whom she was blood-related.

"I don't know Liku."

"Yes, Miss Barbara, you do. You and I passed Liku on the path to visit her farm. She had a bundle of firewood on her back."

"I don't remember her."

"You also know her son. You saw his cattle. You said his cattle made you sad."

Before I could ask her who Liku's son was, I heard Ili's mother calling her from her *bure*, a short distance down the path.

"*So mothe*, Miss Barbara!"

I missed Ili the very second she ran home. She was always quietly concerned and helpful. In addition to the inactivity, the silence of the jungle pressing close, and the sun melting the tin roof over my bed, I was drenched in sweat and my damned foot was no better than it had been two days ago. I fought back tears. Feeling sorry for myself was definitely a big, disgraceful NO! So much work still to do. The sick calf that had put me in this soggy bed needed Richard, the HQ vet. I decided to send a note with Ili to her village school to give to her teacher. She would give the note to a bus driver, who would give it to the local town's agricultural officer. If the one telephone was working, an HQ vet in Suva might come to look at my cattle. He might come next week. He might also decide it wasn't worth an entire day lost in the bush. All the vets were infected with Brucellosis and had to take life easy. Next week I would rope the calf again with the help of at least two farmers.

On the third day in bed there was a faint knock on the door and I called, "*Laco mei, laco mei,* come in, whoever you are!"

A small, misshapen woman peered uncertainly into my *bure* and said, "*Bula bula*, Miss Barbara, *au na Liku au na Liku.*"

Before stepping inside, Liku backed up to a bench outside the door and eased down a bulky bundle of firewood that had been tied to her back. It looked as if it weighed as much as she did. When she stepped inside, the hump on her back was still there. She could not straighten up. Her spine was acutely bent forward and also a bit sideways. Liku was not much to look at. Wrinkled, scaly gray black skin hung loosely over a bony frame.

She came over to my bed and without a word smiled down on me. And what a smile! With her toothless smile, her head tilted sideways to compensate for her crooked spine, I found it easy to smile back.

Liku must have washed herself in the stream before coming, because her grimy tattered *sulu* was dripping wet. Her close-cut frizzy gray hair glistened with drops of water.

Liku spoke only the local dialect, and half her mumbled narration was lost to me. When she found I couldn't understand her, she smiled and repeated several "vinakas" thank-yous. I tried to explain the accident to her, and she mumbled softly, "*Ca, ca, bulamacow, bulamacow*," bad cattle. Liku nodded while silently looking down at my feet. Slowly her fingers began to palpate every part of the ankle, foot, and toes of the good leg before doing the same with the injured one. The pressure she applied was firm as she carefully probed every swollen toe. She didn't miss any of the fifty or whatever throbbing bones in my foot, and to my surprise, her rough-skinned hands were gentle and she didn't add to the pain.

Liku clapped her hands and smiled down on me. "*Sega a kaca, vanaka, vanaka*." Nothing broken.

I sincerely hoped her bush diagnosis had credibility. All I really knew about her was from Ili. Liku helped bring babies into the world. She firmly grasped the tip of each toe with the fingers of one hand, held the adjacent bone with the other hand, and pulled. At first she pulled gently and finally with pressure and massage. I winced and then groaned. Liku ignored my complaints. She continued this process until every bony digit had been pulled, realigned, and massaged. I could feel a warm softening and relaxing in the foot.

Her fingers were surprisingly flexible; though workworn, they looked quite normal, with no arthritic knobs. Whatever had crippled her spine might be congenital or possibly due to an accident in her adult life. Up here in the hills, many hours from help, most accidents went untreated. I had been told during orientation that I could be airlifted out by helicopter, but it had better be a life-threatening injury.

Liku knelt down beside my head, smiled broadly, clapped her hands, and said, "*Lako, lako.*"

She wanted me to get up and walk. I tried a few steps to the door and back, and the pain was certainly now bearable. I was tempted to hug this old woman, but in her culture touching with affection was taboo. I walked gingerly in a small circle on my soft *imbe* mat babbling childlike, "*rai rai vinakas*," beautiful, beautiful.

Liku untied a cloth bag on my worktable and fingered an assortment of medicinal leaves. She mumbled something while looking into my eyes with a serious expression. She wanted me to understand. With pantomine and a few familar words she said that she had picked these leaves in the morning after the sun had drawn potent fluids up from the roots to the plant. She lit my kerosene burner and set a pot of water to boil. After the leaves simmered into a mushy pulp, my *bure* filled with a spicy aroma. I wanted to know the names of all these plants, but she waved me away impatiently, saying, "*Vuni, vuni*," meaning "secret."

Liku spooned the steaming glop from the pot into a towel and motioned me to lie down on the floor. She wrapped the steaming poultice around my foot and tied it in on with string. Padding around looking for something on my shelves, she found my only precious possessions, and before I could get out the right words she unwrapped several plastic bags that protected my camera lenses from glass-scarring tropical molds.

Liku wrapped the plastic bags around the poultice to keep it hot and from leaking onto the *imbe*. Then Liku sat back on her heels and viewed the ungainly lumpy mound that was a foot. She clapped her hands together and laughed. Her laugh had a lyric tone, and it was contagious. The gaping toothless black cavern of her mouth showed naught but a red tongue. "*Ni mataka, ni mataka, bulamacow.*" Tomorrow the cows, tomorrow go back to work.

Thoughts of going back to work tomorrow might be premature, but this was a good time to ask Liku the name of her son and locate her farm. I pointed to my hand-drawn map tacked to the bamboo wall identifying twenty-one farms by numbers and initials of the men's names. Most of their family names were hard for me to remember and pronounce; some had as many as five syllables. Next to the map was a list of all the farmers' names written in block letters. Liku stood in front of the scheme map and with her finger touched each name. She faced me with a puzzled smile.

I asked, "*Nomu luve-na*, your son, Liku, your son?"

She looked at the list of names again and shook her head. She was embarrassed. If Liku was illiterate, she had lots of company. Ili told me her own grandfather and father still signed documents with an X. The cattle scheme had the shape of a slender, elongated eggplant. To Liku, the map must have looked like a meaningless, ridiculous drawing. In the morning Ili would solve the riddle of where Liku's farm was and surely know the name of her son.

Liku was not finished with her bush medicine. She rummaged through my shelves until she found a bottle of coconut oil and gave her hands a good soaking. Then she told me to turn over on my stomach, placed a pillow under the bandaged foot, and proceeded to give me a full body massage. Starting with my healthy foot, she worked upward to my head. With her strong fingers she slowly massaged every joint, muscle, tendon, and ligament. For the first time in this alien and uncomfortable land my body blissfully relaxed, and this old scarecrow of a woman was responsible. I couldn't find the words to tell her this. Instead I mumbled, *"Vaka vina vinaka"* (I am grateful, thank you).

Liku massaged the taut muscles of my neck. Deftly separating tangled hair, she soothingly massaged my scalp with circular motions. Her fingers tenderly stroked my forehead and temples. Liku's caressing hands brought shimmering visions of my mother's arms comforting me after a childhood hurt. I was light as air, my body floating above the jungle canopy. Was this aroma therapy? More of Liku's bush medicine? My eyes were heavy and I slept.

I awoke and it was dark and the night-biting mosquitoes were drawing my blood. I felt immediately guilty that I had not in some meaningful way thanked this humble woman. I wanted her to know I would never forget her. I got into bed and tucked the mosquito netting under the foam mattress. I concentrated on Liku, fixing her every trait into my memory. Many years later, I wanted to be able to remember Liku just as she was on that day, to clearly recall the image of her smiling and quizzical face with wrinkles deep as scars. And her twisted, collapsed spine? Why not bury the cruel reality of her physical ugliness and remember only her lyric laugh, her generosity, and her grace? *What rot,* I decided. *Doesn't work at all. Take away the reality of her damaged body and then it couldn't possibly be Liku.*

Ili said I had completed a farm report on Liku's son's cattle and that his cattle had made me sad. There were a hundred cattle in terrible stages of malnutrition, and they all made me sad. I tried to keep careful farm reports with details to help identify the farmer with his cattle. For some reason I could not remember Liku's son or the location of his farm. He must have no children for Liku to work as hard as she did gathering firewood. I decided I must do something special for Liku and her son. Blissfully sleepy, for the first time in too many days I felt peacefully.

8
Akariva versus Constructive Ambiguities

The morning after Liku worked her bush medicine on me, I overslept several hours. Ili was long gone to her village school, and I wasn't quite ready to risk walking down the path to Maria's *bure* to ask her where Liku and her son's farm was. There was also a good possibility Maria was illiterate and wouldn't be able to read the names of the twenty-one farmers or locate them on my map.

When I opened my front door, the sun was high in the sky and down the path Maria was bent low sweeping her *imbe* lying on the ground. She made brooms out of soft twigs tied with vines around a short club shaved smooth with her machete. She had made a broom for me, but every time I swept with it my back complained. I wanted to explain the design flaw to her, but all over Fiji women used the same short-handled brooms to sweep out their homes. Somehow I couldn't bring myself to ask her the question: "Why don't you use a long-handled broom so you can stand upright?" The question would have sounded like an insult to Maria. For thousands of years these brooms had been made exactly the same way.

I watched Maria, and when she straightened up to rub her lower back she saw me, waved and called, *"Rai rai vinaka, yave na?"* (Your foot is good?)

I waved back and Maria again bent low over her sweeping. My job description referred only to *bulamacows*, not correcting design flaws of the Fijian broom.

During the next few days this job description took an unwilling and alarming jump into the sale of timber and a boundary dispute. Before Fiji became a British colony, most of those bloody tribal conflicts had been rooted in questions of land ownership or chiefly lineage. Kona reported that a violent confrontation had occurred between two farmers after too many hours of *yanqona* drinking. The news was chilling.

Two farmers on the scheme both sold valuable hardwood trees to a lumber company in Suva. One large tree was felled by Indian loggers, and the Indian forester, who estimated board feet of felled trees, credited the money to Mosese. Akariva, a neighbor of Mosese, insisted the tree was on his property, so the money was his and not Mosese's.

"Kona, why not have your father and the village elders settle this quarrel?"

"My father says this is a cattle scheme problem. The money for the trees is supposed to go to the bank to pay off loans. He says this is the *bulamacow* lady's job."

"Tell your father I'm not a trained negotiator. I don't know Mosese very well, only that he has some of the best cows because he has the best pastures close to the river. Akariva, I don't even remember him. Your father must do this. It sounds too serious to muck up."

"My father says you know how to do this."

"Kona, I'm the one who feels I cannot, dare not, do this. I'm sorry; I can't."

"My father says he saw your degree at your university had a major in political science. He says politicians know how to make compromises."

"Kona, yes, that was one of my majors, but I am not a politician. I have no negotiating skills. Ask Suni; he will verify that diplomacy, a lack of, is my major character flaw."

"Miss Barbara, it is too late. My father sent a message to Akariva to meet you. I will also be here to translate if Akariva doesn't understand your Fijian."

Kona smiled broadly when he teased me. He never missed an opportunity to laugh at my use of his language. He accused me of speaking Fijian with an "ingrown tongue." Only he knew what he meant by that. When he left me and walked down the path to his village he had a self-satisfied smile on his open young face. I found it impossible not to like this youngster. When his father died and Kona was chief, how was he going to keep order in his village with his carefree approach to life? Perhaps as well as his tough old warrior father. No one could deny his charm and intelligence.

Cleverly Chief Siti had placed me in an unpleasant position, keeping himself far away from a dangerous feud. If I lost control over the feud, the burden would be mine and never his. He tolerated me only for the money and cattle I brought to his cattle scheme.

I had never made decisions as to who sold timber, only offered advice on preventing clear cutting and slash-and-burn tactics. Several times the young Indian forester, who spoke English like a Brit, asked me to be present when he measured board feet of timber. I had thought surely he was merely being polite. Wrong again. Apparently, I was also responsible for collecting information on whose timber was cut, the total board feet, and how much money each farmer received.

I assumed wrongly that the Indian was just one more civil servant merely following guidelines of all those redundant forms in triplicate. I had no experience in the business of logging and wanted no part of it. The sight of giant ancient trees being dragged out of the woods by a team of oxen, leaving behind deep muddy ravines, was a distressing one. The expression "raping the land" was truth in this case, and it was the Fijian who gave the Indians permission to do so.

The morning Akariva was scheduled to come to my *bure* started badly with news on the grapevine telephone that a four-day-old calf had a high temperature. The cow died after delivering, and her calf missed out on the lifesaving colostrum. This first milk gives calves immune-fighting antibodies, a powerful weapon in their new environment, a dirty, contaminated pasture. A high temperature in a new calf often means fatal pneumonia. The time element was important, and I wanted to start the calf on penicillin shots as soon as possible. The calf wasn't too far away, and I was anxious to get started.

I sat on the bench outside my door and waited for Akariva. Try as I did, I couldn't remember him. Where was Ili when I needed her? She knew every family name of twenty-one men, who was neighbor to whom, and who was blood-related, right down to third cousins.

A tall, angular man finally came into view and yes. I finally remembered a man who spoke next to no English and during the entire site visit kept an unfriendly silence, not a happy man. During several site visits I made to his hilly farm he never showed up at all.

Akariva's gait was a jerking one, so different from the flowing stride of most Fijian men in the bush. I watched as he stepped off the path and with his machete cut open a heavy vine. Immediately liquid poured out as if from a water hose. Akariva turned his face up to it and had a long drink. A farmer had told me how to recognize this vine in case I ever needed clean water to drink on my trips into the bush. The liquid tasted and looked like water.

I walked toward Akariva and held out my hand.

"Akariva, *bula, bula*; thank you for coming."

I did not ask him into my *bure* for the traditional rest with a cup of tea. I was in a hurry. This was a serious mistake. To him, not being offered simple hospitality was insulting. He came for conversation with a white woman he didn't want to talk with; he was tired and sweating after a long walk in the heat and expected me to serve him tea. But I had another reason for my inhospitality; I felt it imprudent to sit alone with a man inside my *bure*—even with all three doors open. Kona had also indicated that Akariva had a short fuse.

Gazing into Akariva's face gave me an unpleasant jolt. His dry black skin was scaly, probably due to too much *yanqona* drinking. His deep-set eyes glowered in a jagged, asymmetrical face.

My plan was to begin offering him something that I was not going to offer Mosese. If Chief Siti told me to begin negotiations with Akariva, the reason was that he was the more truculent of the two men.

"Akariva, your cattle could use a new bull. It may take a month or so, but a new bull will upgrade your herd in the years to come. What do you think?"

"*Vanaka, vanaka.*" His thank-you was a growl mumbled through heavy, dry lips. His eyes remained downcast.

"I wish every farmer could have a new bull, but we don't have the money."

Akariva listened in silence, concentrating on tracing circles in the dust with his machete. Maybe he didn't understand me. Slowly I repeated the message, keeping my eyes on the circles growing larger on the ground and away from his ugly and immobile face. I had no problem, whatsoever, remembering that looking a man in the eye is an act of aggression or an invitation for intimacy.

"Looking over the last report, I can report to HQ that your cattle are in good-enough condition to merit a new bull."

I lied. His cows were between grade two and three and his grasses had low nutritional value and the surrounding bush was sparse. Whoever was responsible for recommending cattle on this farm was having a *yanqona* fantasy. Ili had said his cows made me sad. I recalled walking home after a site visit with an image I could not shake: cows with their "hooks," their pelvic bones, sticking out sharply and ribs protruding through diseased hides.

I felt helpless, not knowing what to do. I never had seen his home. He probably did not have a wife; who in God's Fiji would marry this grotesque man?

"Akariva, I can sell your old bull at the abattoir, perhaps get close to one hundred dollars, get you a new bull, free. The tree that was logged is worth about one hundred and will go to Mosese. You will get a new bull plus one hundred for the old bull."

"Mosese getting new bull?"

"I don't know quite yet."

"Mosese gets new bull, then I take one. The tree money is mine."

His thinking made no sense to me. He was homely as sin but not stupid. He was asking far too much; he wasn't playing the negotiating game. I was lost over the puzzle of his interest in Mosese getting a new bull. Why did Akariva care? He was getting one. The sun was hot, I was losing patience, and in the tropics a four-day-old sick calf gets sicker by the minute. I must get the penicillin to the calf.

Akariva's machete sped up. Frenetically he drew jagged lines in the dust. Discouraged, I stared at his dusty gray crusting and splayed feet. I was relieved to hear a clear young voice calling my name from the path to the village.

"*Bula*, Akariva; *bula*, Miss Barbara! I heard you might need help with a sick calf."

Kona was always perceptive and could see that our conversation was not going well. He said something to Akariva in the local dialect that I didn't understand; I only heard him mention Chief Siti's name. Whatever it was, Akariva made no response. In English I brought Kona up-to-date on my failed attempt to settle the dispute.

"Miss Barbara, even if you give him two bulls, it will not replace the lost tree money."

My patience was at an end. I raised my arms and looked directly into Akariva's eyes and then into Kona's. My words came out brisk and blunt.

"If he receives a new bull and Mosese does not, he will not lose face. He will also be getting twice the value of the tree in a new bull, plus the money from the old. The sire of the next shipment of bulls is from a famous bloodline of bulls in New Zealand. For goodness' sake, we are talking big money here. Kona, tell this to him, and now."

"I will tell him, but—"

Kona spoke slowly to Akariva in the local dialect, and I watched the latter's face. His eyes shifted with startling speed from Kona's face to mine. When he learned that Mosese was to be credited with the tree, his jaw quivered. He squared his shoulders and faced me, tensing every sinewy muscle in his body. His black eyes stared aggressively into mine, and his harsh voice exploded in my face.

"Tree belongs to me."

My voice shrilled, "Akariva, be sensible, please!"

Akariva never touched me, but the violent force of his anger hurled me backward. I gasped for breath and with the rush of adrenaline my hands and legs quivered. Some powerful force from him cut into me. I regained my footing and tried to compose myself. Within a fraction of a second Akariva had became the instant killer of past generations. In his fury the corners of his mouth pulled his lips open to show yellowing teeth and his craggy face contorted into that of a menacing animal.

I saw the hand gripping his machete lifting and heard Kona shouting. "*Akariva, senga, senga*! No, no!"

Kona's shout echoed back to us from the hills. He grabbed Akariva's arms and spoke to him again. Akariva's face twisted in helpless confusion, and his body slumped. He averted his eyes from ours. His head jerking defiantly, he turned and walked stiffly up the path toward his farm. We watched as he lifted his machete and slashed at bushes on both sides of the path.

Somewhere in the bamboo dust of my *bure* lay a soggy pack of cigarettes. I had given up this drug a few months ago. It had been so easy I bragged to my friend in a letter: "If I can do it living without running water and electricity while muddling through a hundred frustrations every day, so can you." But that was before one tree had been felled.

Smoking the vile, damp drug required concentration. The cigarettes kept going out. Relighting with shaking hands was a challenge. Matches in the tropics are never completely dry. I needed time to find logic in what had just happened.

Diplomacy and improvisation had failed dismally. I had failed and, worse, lost my temper. I might have been killed if Kona, the chiefly young son of Siti, had not been at my side. And now Akariva was without a doubt capable of murdering Mosese with his machete. It was too easy. He would sneak up on Mosese at night in his *bure* or find him alone in the bush tending his cattle and slash his throat. The whole grisly episode played out before my eyes.

But was it all my fault? Something was missing, a fact overlooked, a fact misinterpreted, a cultural snag not honored.

I glanced out the door and saw Kona sitting cross-legged on a grassy mound facing the direction in which Akariva had gone. I joined Kona and he looked at my cigarette. I offered him the crumpled package. He took one and it went limp in his fingers. He whispered a "Vanaka," and tried to stuff the lumpy cigarette back in the wrapper.

We sat solemnly staring into the green hills. Kona was strangely silent. Possibly for the first time in his young life he had used his chiefly position and power. I didn't want to think about what Akariva might or might not have done to me if I had been alone. Kona and I knew the feud between Akariva and Mosese would now accelerate. The peace of an entire cattle scheme was in jeopardy.

Only one hour ago Kona had been a confident and carefree youth. Now he sat tense and alert, his face averted from mine. And it had been brought about by that inept white woman. The same woman who couldn't handle the ceremonial *yanqona* but had fallen into the *tanoa* bowl and insulted his culture.

I had been overconfident. Akariva was now doubly wounded, and I did not have a clue why. It had all looked so easy. Now the sin of pride peeled away from me, leaving me feeling ill. It was probably the moldy cigarettes.

"Kona, shouldn't we warn Mosese?"

"I must leave and speak to my father first. He will make the decision."

The chief! He had no sympathy for me; he merely used me.

"Kona, why? Why? Akariva was getting so much more than Mosese, why?"

Kona hesitated a moment. "Mosese is Akariva's half brother. They have the same father."

Ah! The missing fact: a wounded heart. May all theories be damned.

"Akariva's father left him and his mother many years ago to take a young new wife. Akariva's mother was relieved. Her husband had beaten her and broken her spine. This is still happening in our country. The farm was divided, with Akariva's father getting the best part of the land close to the river. That is why Mosese and his father's grass is good and the cattle fat. The new family prospers while Akariva and his mother struggle. They are always a little hungry. His mother looks seventy and is only forty years old."

"I have not met Akariva's mother."

Kona glared at me and shouted, "You have! You have! The old woman who came to you when you hurt your foot and you could not walk. She gave you massage and bush medicine."

"Liku, that frail old woman with the twisted spine? The one who is always carrying firewood strapped to her back? Dear God, why was I not told this?"

Kona shouted, "Because you are an outsider! You are not family! You will always be a stranger to us. Miss Barbara you should know this by now."

He turned his back to me. A few minutes ago Akariva, in his fury, had lifted his machete to me, and now Kona had denounced me as a stranger and not family. When Orisi adopted me as his daughter, he made me family and miraculously I actually felt like family, until this morning, after one tree had been cut down. The problem, the bigoted

Fijian cultural enigma of having only two classes of relationships, excluding the one of friend, was harsh and hurtful and all-controlling.

The night after Akariva's violent outburst was destined to be a sleepless one. Under my mosquito net I heard familiar rustling sounds on the floor mats, but I could not rouse myself, turn on the flashlight, and terminate one more rat with a rock from my pile beside my bed. Even the nightly chase, the rat kill, palled. A malaise engulfed me. Let the rats have their way in my cupboards. They were here first. In this culture I was the outsider. The rats were family.

Liku had come to me in my need, and today this was how I had rewarded her. Tonight Liku was lying in her dirty falling-down *bure* knowing the tree money would not go to her son. Did she accept the decision of an outsider as one more insult to her only child? How would Liku react? Would the gnawing bitterness in Akariva's heart also find a home in his mother's?

Mother and son lay under the same rusting tin roof of their shack, but would Liku remember that her son had been conceived, a very long time ago, in a moment of love? I always found the Fijian women quaint in their use of the word *magic*, the word meaning *sex*. Envisioning Akariva, glum and ugly, conceived in a moment of *magic* was a sad bit of irony. The hatred Akariva felt toward his half brother had a long history and needed only a spark to ignite. Destiny had never given Akariva and his mother a leg-up. The feud had to be taken seriously. Even in these remote hills a breakdown in marriage vows took a heavy toll on children.

In the Western world, property boundaries are based on benchmarks and with the use of laser-assisted survey equipment legal descriptions are an exacting procedure.

Not in Fiji. In rough, undulating jungle, plats and metes are measured by walking barefoot over property, using trees or rocks as boundary markers. The scenario for disaster is endless. Borders ebb and flow. Marker trees die, rocks dislodge into ravines, and barbed wire is thrown around any convenient sapling. Boundaries are faulty memories paced off on top of ridges or in ravines. A volcanic island has little else other than hills and ravines. Which ones?

There were daily events of wandering cattle's disrespect for strands of barbed wire draped casually between and around trees. I had counted the same cow with three tits on several farms. The men tolerated visiting cows. But if a cow from another village became a permanent resident, the adoption procedure included a stealthy slaughter and a quiet feast with only close family members invited. If the breezes carried the rare aroma of sizzling beef to the rightful owner and evidence was found, then a murderous encounter was inevitable.

Placing a bull in any but the best-managed herds was a waste. Placing one in Akariva's herd was not a good cattle management practice, even if he was able to upgrade his grass. My decision was based solely on keeping peace. If Mosese was as well off as Kona indicated, this might be an opportunity to ask him to open his riverfront pasture to Akariva. Mosese had more grass than he needed. He was the younger son. We could discuss this together. I could, without any guilt, also give Mosese a bull. Faces may yet be saved—worth a try. The situation was too serious to quibble about a couple of hundred dollars. Suni didn't give a damn, and Richard would concur. Every month he gave me more latitude to make decisions.

It was Akariva with whom I had to deal. It would be Akariva who would kill Mosese the next time he found him alone. They were neighbors, so it would be very soon.

He would then spend the rest of his life in prison, and Liku would be doubly shamed.

Very few island men join their spirit ancestors without a machete scar or two. "How many wounds are caused by farmers accidentally slashing flesh and how many originate by fighting?" is an apt question. A Fijian man, composed and placid one minute, can with lightning speed erupt into a furious conflict. Very few want to ask the question: is it in the genes or is it learned behavior? I didn't have a clue, and even if I did, it wouldn't solve the problem at hand.

A rustle and a squeal announced two rats fighting. With rock in one hand, the flashlight clicking on in the other, my aim found the varmint. I scored! One anguished squeal and then silence. Hot damn! That felt good. Tonight I needed to kill that one rat.

I got out of bed, lit the benzene lantern, and stood in front of my map of the cattle scheme and muttered, "Constructive ambiguities!" Three thousand acres of constructive ambiguities. And until one tree was logged it had all worked so nicely. Up to now the only problem was lumber companies that forgot to pay for the removed logs, with either money or delivery of milled lumber for home building.

I gathered up my scheme maps and current farm reports and crawled back into bed and under the mosquito netting. Sure enough, that crazy tree was on Mosese's farm but not by too much. My first task after coming to this job was to draw a large map outlining twenty-one farms on the 3,000-acre *matangali*, village-owned land. The map on graph paper was not precise but accurate enough. How often did farmers go to HQ to examine files? Never! They were refused entry by Indian file clerks who took advantage of the situation to pull rank. No freedom-of-information laws in third world countries. A little gerrymandering on new graph paper was clearly in order. Is this what Chief Siti and future Chief Kona would approve to avoid trouble on the scheme? Absolutely! That is, if they found out.

Operating on the premise that Liku, Akariva, and Mosese would be nicely buried in hallowed ground beside their revered ancestors by the time my improbity surfaced, the rest was as easy as sending a message at daybreak via jungle telephone. One more meeting: Mother Liku, Akariva, Kona sitting on my Sunday best *imbe* mat, teapot and biscuits in place. Better still, there is a can of fish to open. Up here in the hills, fish is a luxury. Ili's mother can bring me some cooked *dalo*. Practically a feast. And before getting down to business we'd look through my mini–photo album of my family and linger over photos of my well-conditioned Aberdeen Angus grazing on verdant green pastures. We'd have a relaxed visit. Yanqona? Forget it! Everybody sober. Cultural mandates go hang.

With two men present, Liku would crouch in the corner, silent but alert. Her eyes would be on the floor. I would treat her as a friend, serving her food before serving the men, not like in her culture. Out of the hearing of others Liku was undoubtedly the authority figure in the life of Akariva. Without a doubt Liku had up to now kept a lid on her son's smoldering jealousy.

When getting down to business, I would propose Akariva split the proceeds of the tree with his half brother. Akariva would get a new bull and sell his old bull and instead of paying off his debt at the bank, give Akariva the money. If Akariva still showed anger at sharing the tree money with his half brother, I could give him the entire proceeds and his face would be saved from another insult to his "elder brother" status. The more prosperous Mosese I hoped would prove less volatile. After the meeting I would send a message to Mosese to come to a meeting, with the future Chief Kona present. If Mosese showed a measure of discontent at having lost half the proceeds of the tree to his older brother, and I would stress "older brother," he also gets a new bull. He would then be shown the new scheme map and told the tree had never belonged to him. That should save the younger brother his face in the dispute.

Ethical negotiations be hanged! Long live improvisation and mendacity.

9
Too Many Babies and No Calves

How do I get rid of a baby?

Stunned, I stared silently at the words on a lined page from a school workbook. This, the most difficult question in the world in any culture, was not what I had been led to expect from school children. I was sitting in a *bure* at night surrounded by thirteen teenage girls on the most remote farm of the cattle scheme. There was no way in heaven or hell I could address these questions simplistically.

My jungle grapevine telephone didn't reach this isolated village. So I had simply showed up one morning expecting to spend the night in the home of the village chief or a member of his family.

After dinner I was confronted with a request by school principal Lania to speak to her older girls. What should have been a harmless little after-dinner pastime, evolved into a "let us take this rare opportunity to pick this American lady's brain." Principal Lania, one of the most attractive and sophisticated women I had met in this country, had set me up. Only someone as intelligent as Lania, a woman ready to face hard decisions head-on, could have provided me with one of the more distressing memories in my life. Lania had no forewarning of my site visit. When I arrived at her village she was teaching her morning class. By the time I finished eating my supper her plan was put into action.

There were several farms to visit in Sote Village, which was more than a two-or-three-hour hike from my *bure*. There were several hills and valleys to cross. Sote had its own school, and the only method of transportation to the cities was by bamboo raft or the one outboard motor skiff on the largest river in Fiji, the Rewa.

By midmorning I had walked to the crest of a grassy hill and gazed down on Sote, remote and untouched by the grime and dissonance of a city. I slid my knapsack off my shoulders and sat awhile to rest. The scene lifted my spirits. Every *bure* shimmered in the sunlight with a clean thatched roof and carefully plaited bamboo walls. This village was healthy and flourishing. Bright flowering hibiscus shrubs surrounded the village green, the grass as carefully tended as on a golf course in Suva, only here it was cut with a machete. A row of papaw trees heavy with ripening fruit sheltered under large leaves, encircled the village.

I thought of the French Impressionist Gauguin, sitting in my place watching the glow and sparkle of the stream surrounding this enchanted village like a protective moat. On the far side of the village the stream emptied into the immense and fast-moving Rewa River. Several women with their *sulus* wrapped only around their waists were leisurely draping their laundry over shrubs outside their *bures*. I could hear their soft voices floating up to me as they moved through their daily chores with a carefree grace—no need to hurry, no intrusion from the outside world, my world that whizzed and careened through every crisis in order to prepare for the next. This village thrived in a time warp, one hundred, two hundred, or more years without a change. If Gauguin had seen this village first, might he not have stayed here instead of settling in Tahiti? From where I sat, looking down on Sote, the village looked to be a magical place. I was going to enjoy my two-day stay in this charming pristine village.

At the water's edge of the stream, with only the cows watching, I took all my clothes off and wrapped a *sulu* around myself. Balancing my knapsack on my head with clothing and boots inside, I waded across and scrambled up the muddy embankment.

The cattle grazing the lush grasses along the stream were the best-looking I'd seen all month. In fact, they did my heart good just gazing at them. Some were downright fat. From this isolated village the men and women took their produce to market in Suva on bamboo rafts, drifting with the current. Getting home again took an entire day by bus and many hours of walking through the bush. Farmers spent their days working on their farms, with only rare trips to the cities.

Slogging, dripping wet, toward the village, I found many *vale lailai* were graced with frangipangi and other sweetly aromatic plants. No standing in line for the morning necessities in this pretty village. It was not the first time I had reported on this farm, but the last time I had Maria's eldest daughter to guide me and she spent so much time socializing on the way in the *bures* of her extended family that by the time we arrived at Sote little time was left to see the cattle or get to know the farmers and their wives. Alone this time, I would be able to make a more thorough site visit.

At the first *bure* I knocked on the door frame and when the lady of the house came to the door and saw me in my wet *sulu* and mud-covered boots she laughed.

"*Bula*, Miss Barbara, *laco mai, laco mai*. Give me your boots."

Who else in all the world could it be but the *bulamacow* lady working on the cattle scheme? Ducking behind a curtained area, I put on my dry clothes, and my hostess draped my *sulu* over a bush to dry. My unfamiliar *sulu*, which was really a sheet I had torn in half, got the attention of several women who soon appeared and called out their welcome. Before I could get settled, one of the women told me to follow her to the largest *bure* in the village and to the home of the cheerful and opulent Gowena. Her *sulu* was a print of oversize orchids in brilliant hues no orchid breeder would attempt to grow. Gowena enjoyed wearing *sulus* that dazzled. Out of respect to me she adjusted her dazzling *sulu* to cover her undulating and bouncing bosom. Obviously Gowena had been shopping in Suva. One hundred years ago Gowena would have been draped in a stiff black-and-white *sulu* made from the mulberry tree bark pounded into unyielding cloth. Even then Gauguin, who loved only voluptuous women, would have fallen for Gowena in a big way.

Gowena welcomed me with a wide smile. "Miss Barbara, come and sit and we will have tea. You can rest while we wait for my husband. They are calling him now."

Her *bure* was bright and clean, and aluminum cooking pots, lined up on bamboo shelves outside, glistened in the sun. On a shelf over the front door, out of harm's way, the lady of the house displayed a bone china teapot and cups and saucers. Culturally rooted in past centuries, Gowena also enjoyed the present.

In English she said, "Miss Barbara, we didn't know you were coming, but you are so very welcome. No one has come to see our farms since your last visits."

"How does it happen you speak English so well?"

"I had one year at the University of the South Pacific, but my older sister, Lania, graduated. She is now principal of our village school."

"Is her husband also a *bulamacow* farmer?"

"Yes, of course, just like my husband."

Several of the women brought hot tea and thick slices of papaw. This was always a treat, and I said, "I can never get enough of your papaws. They grow as large as a football in your country. In mine they're the size of a pear."

Gowena's laugh was lusty. "You Americans are all the same. Mrs. Eleanor Roosevelt came to Suva during the war and papaw was also her favorite fruit. My parents took ours to market on the rafts, and the cook at the governor's mansion told us she had them every day for breakfast."

"Mrs. Roosevelt came to Fiji?"

"More than once. She loved our country, and there were many American soldiers here, and even more sailors. Her chauffeur still lives in Suva and tells many wonderful stories about her. Now he is old, but he still drives for our government. When Mrs. Roosevelt came there were many, many warships in Suva, and too-many-to-count fighter planes in Nandi."

"Did you ever meet her yourself?"

"No, I was just a baby then. My father met her. He said she was a very friendly lady."

Gowena's husband, Tiko, came in and sat down next to his wife. He was over six feet tall, with not an ounce of body fat. He didn't have the typical halo-style haircut; his hair was cut to the scalp. Like most Fijian farmers, he didn't have much willingness for conversation. Information would have to be gathered with my eyes.

He and I walked over his grassland for over an hour without talking. His cow numbers were correct, but he didn't have enough calves. The bull was in reasonably good condition, so what was the problem? Calves dying shortly after birth might mean a vitamin A deficiency. Another reason is every cattleperson's worst nightmare: Brucellosis, undulant fever. There is no cure. The cattle must be slaughtered. Tiko shrugged his shoulders in answer to the question, "Do you find premature calves being born dead?" Tiko himself was a study in enigmatic behavior. Was he possibly chronically sick or was this simply Tiko? For a tall, slender, fit-looking man he moved too slowly, his every move economical. He also walked like a man who didn't feel well and hadn't for a long time.

Withdrawing blood samples from these cattle for testing and keeping the specimens refrigerated on the long trip to the lab was going to be a hard task. A British vet in Suva told me that in northern rural England a large number of patients in an asylum for the mentally ill had tested positive for Brucellosis. For this terrible disease to appear in Sote would be a tragedy. It was highly contagious. Finding one victim meant finding many more.

Later I planned to ask Gowena and the other women if they boiled their milk. In this village where did they get milk for the children other than from their own cows? Beni certainly should have reported on this low calving rate. How could he have been so negligent?

On the way back to Gowena's *bure* I was tempted to ask Tiko if he was the chief of this village, but an inner voice told me this question might be an unwelcome one to this quiet man. Just outside his door he surprised me with a request.

"Miss Barbara, please take this sixty dollars and deposit in my loan account in the bank."

Before I could stop Tiko, he shoved a dirty, crumpled packet of bills into my hand. I hadn't planned a trip into Suva for several weeks, and this was considered big money in Fiji. This could be his yearly income. Expatriates had had their throats cut for less than this. I never carried more than a few dollars on me, so I hesitated to take it. In the past

Beni had been given money to take to the bank for the farmers in just this way. How easy it was for him to simply forget to bank the money. And how hard it would be to learn just how much he had kept for himself over a period of only a few years. Bookkeeping in Suni's office was still in the dark ages. I decided if no one but Tiko knew I had the money I would be safe until I got to Suni's HQ and placed it under lock and key.

Inside the *bure* sat a middle-aged woman, lighter-skinned than Gowena. A flawless beauty in any culture, she had more than a drop of white blood running in her veins and she was wearing makeup. Her dress was a sedate navy blue with delicate white edging, and she was the only villager wearing shoes.

Gowena introduced me to her older sister, Lania, the school principal. There was a studied elegance and grace in Lania's manner, with none of the hearty spontaneity of her younger sister. She studied me, watched me, did not initiate a conversation, did not rise from her sitting position on the *imbe*, and did not offer her hand in greeting. She either considered me her equal or considered herself my superior. I wondered if this might not be a clever, even a shrewd woman. I understood that in Lania's eyes I was very much a stranger. Had she heard that I was the adopted daughter of Orisi? It occurred to me that her own father could have adopted me and I would still be a stranger to her.

I knelt down across from Lania and opened my knapsack to take out my notebook so I could fill out the farm reports. There was no notebook inside. Then I saw that it lay beside Lania. Had I left it out of my knapsack when I left with Tiko? I didn't think so. That notebook had the highest priority of all my possessions. I searched her face for an answer as I reached for my notebook.

Finally she spoke. "Barbara, I took the liberty of glancing at your farm reports. You take a great deal of information into account when visiting our farms. Beni never asked us any of these questions. In fact, he hasn't looked at our cattle in a very long time."

"I'm surprised that you're interested in record keeping," I said.

She sounded haughty when she answered, "That is what Beni said when I questioned him. He said it wasn't a woman's concern."

"I'm sorry, Lania; I did not mean to imply—"

"It's time farmers' wives learned to keep financial records for their husbands. They are working hard and their wives can do this when they come in from their gardens. They must learn bookkeeping."

"What did you learn from my reports? Please tell me."

Ignoring my question, she asked, "You are working the cattle scheme by yourself? Where is Beni? He is not doing a good job."

Lania was openly criticizing one of her own countrymen to an outsider. Something was amiss here. She was one pushy teacher. Could it be I was sitting across from the village chief?

"Lania, I really don't know Beni very well. You're a better judge of this man."

Lania's smile was not a warm one when she said, "You are tired, Barbara. Why don't you rest before supper? Gowena will make you feel comfortable here. She has already prepared a bed for you with mosquito netting."

Her next announcement dumbfounded me.

"I have arranged for all the girls from the sixth grade upward to come here tonight after supper for discussion on topics that interest them very much in their young lives."

"And these topics would be?"

"They are maturing and want to ask you how young women in your country meet their husbands and perhaps some questions about having children."

"Surely you have visiting nurses who give your children all their shots and who can do this far better than the *bulamacow* lady."

"Most of these nurses come to us from religious sects. No, you must do this. The girls are expecting you."

It was the second time within minutes that I didn't know what to say to this imperious woman. She might very well be the self-imposed chief of this village. I wanted to tell her frankly that I was just the *bulamacow* lady, who could discuss the estrus cycle of cows far more comfortably than I could discuss the prepubescent sexual desires and needs of her girls.

"Lania, you know your cultural imperatives in raising teenagers and instructing them. I know livestock—that's all—you don't have the right to ask me to discuss family planning. Never have I done this, and I wouldn't know where to begin."

"Barbara, the girls will arrive at seven o'clock tonight. Meeting you will be a unique experience for them. How often do these girls have an opportunity to meet an American woman, a woman who is not afraid to travel alone halfway around the planet to manage a cattle scheme?"

What a strange village. Charming and clean and traditional, everything in its proper order, people generous and innocent, but here was one tough, unyielding spirit sitting across from me. Was I feeling the influence of a powerful black *turanga*, a chief? And this woman was definitely not all Fijian. She could be the child of one white parent. I felt victimized. She had placed me in an impossible and vulnerable position, discussing sex education with young Fijian girls. I was reminded of Chief Siti placing me in the middle of a smoldering feud between Akariva and Mosese. Always being pawn in the hands of village chiefs was getting to be wearing.

Within a few hours I was sitting next to a composed Lania and greeting a group of young giggling girls holding sheets of paper.

How do I get rid of a baby?

The question was written in large block letters on lined school paper. I read and reread, anything to delay raising my face to these wide-eyed young girls sitting cross-legged in a semicircle in front of Lania and me. By the light of a kerosene lantern hanging from the center of the *bure*, maybe one candlepower, I hoped in vain I had misread.

All the other questions the girls had written on their papers had been nice and easy. "How do American girls meet their future husbands?" "Is it true after marriage the couples live in their own *bures* and not with the man's parents?" "In our country women are not allowed to sleep with their husbands for two years after having a baby. Is it the same with American women?"

I fudged quite a lot on that last one. In fact, I never answered it, only spoke about how nursing a baby for two years did not prevent pregnancy, and so forth and so on.

The last question, terminating a pregnancy, I never expected. This question was as hard as it could possibly get, and people the world over still argue over it. Without glancing at Lania, I dropped the sheet of paper in her lap. If she didn't like my answer, she was free to contribute her own voice. Up to now she had played the part of the silent and alert principal.

I took a deep breath and looked directly at the girls.

"Girls, you have your baby; of course you have your baby. This is the only choice you have when pregnant."

A robust young voice broke the long uncomfortable silence with, "Miss Barbara, we can find *wai-ni-yava*, our bush medicine, to get rid of babies so we do not have to have them."

"Girls, bush medicine is not as safe for you as having your baby. Now do you have any other questions?"

"Miss Barbara, can we make a baby during our periods?"

"The best way is to have no sex, whatsoever; then you will not have babies. You must say no to the man; this is the only way not to have babies."

Never, never had I spoken to my own children in this manner. I covered my anguish with severity in my voice I hardly recognized as my own. These girls were so innocent they had never heard the words *condom* or *diaphragm,* and with all these missionaries in Fiji they never would. These were young girls in a Garden of Eden.

Gowena's home was larger than most, and in the deeper shadows I was surprised to see a young woman, not one of the students, get up from a sitting position and quietly leave. She was a pretty woman and quite large around her waist. She must have come in behind the girls without my seeing her.

Lania finally spoke to the girls, and after many *"vinaka vaka levu,* Miss Barbara, *sa mothe,"* they were gone.

I was exhausted, feeling drained and a little ill. Lania was watching me with a bemused and irritated expression. What a baffling woman.

"Lania, there are no condoms in all of your two hundred islands. What in heaven's name can one tell these girls?"

"You should not have told them not to have any sex at all with their husbands and left it at that. If they do as you suggest, their husbands might beat them or take a second wife if they can afford one. And if they cannot afford to they will sleep with women whose husbands are away working or in Lebanon in the peacekeeping army."

For the first time in this country, I had been criticized by a woman, and I felt insulted and angry. Lania had no right to hold this attitude towards me. She had put me in an impossible position. Her harshness reminded me of Chief Siti. And just where the hell was the chief of this village anyway? As boring as the *yanqona* ceremony was, it was important to know who made all the decisions. In this village who was the chief? Tiko, sleeping behind the curtain in the shadows? He didn't behave like the chief of this village.

"Lania, you know that only rich women, the white women in your country, can have an abortion. And for that they fly to Hawaii or Australia. Surely you know that."

"My husband and I remain close because we have sex every time he wants and every time I want. Always! We have a good marriage."

This was the first time in Fiji I had heard the word *sex* used by a Fijian. Always the metaphors "making magic" or "giving a gift to someone" were used. But never the "S" Word.

Lania's voice softened. "You were right to tell the girls not to use bush medicine. We have old women in villages who use sorcery and *wai-ni-sau-gone*, poisonous herbs, on our girls. Sometimes even crude sharp bamboo tools. Very bad."

"Surely you don't have any babies without fathers in your village, do you?"

"We have two, and it is two more than we have ever had before—this is very rare because we are so far from the city. The men in my village have sex only with their wives."

Again the words *my village* loud and clear, and I asked, "Is that unusual, having babies outside marriage?"

"In my village it has never happened before, no. We are far away from large cities and temptations. But now we have one pregnant woman whose husband has been in Lebanon for two years as a member of the peacekeeping force. She was here tonight. She left us before the girls went home. The young girl who asked the last question is pregnant and is in her last year at school. No! This has never happened before."

"You do not know who the fathers are?"

"I did not say that I do not know."

"I am very sorry, Lania. Will the babies be taken care of?"

"Oh, yes, their father is Fijian and he is a man who came here on farm business. Our village will accept the children. Barbara, I am relieved that you are here now and not him."

The "you are here now and not him" was whispered in a low, conspiratorial voice. There was only one person I was replacing—Beni. The news came in a whisper with the impact of an explosion in my brain.

How to respond to Lania's bombshell? By now I was almost certain she was talking about Beni. Beni had come here on "farm business." Again without absolute proof, I thought about his bringing his own cattle to the scheme for farmers to feed when their own cattle were starving and diseased.

Suddenly there was too much information and all of it damaging to this cattle scheme and to the families. I wanted Lania to leave me. This day had to end. Enough!

Sleep, only sleep. I was angry. I said, "*Lania, sa oti. Finito. Sa mothe.* Good night, please, Lania, good night."

Still on my knees, I moved over to the curtain thrown over a roof beam, lifted it, and found an airfoam mat and a pillow. Lania left immediately. I didn't have the energy to undress before I lay down. A few hours later I woke with every inch of bare skin covered with mosquito bites. I had forgotten to lower the net hanging over me. With a flashlight I rummaged in my knapsack for antiseptic. Every infected bite in the tropics becomes a staph-laden boil that might lead to blood poisoning. When I tucked my knapsack back into a corner I found a *tanoa* bowl, a large one, large enough to belong to a chief. So, by birthright, Tiko was chief. His wife, Gowena, was my hostess because she was the chief's wife. The girls came to this *bure*, the largest one in the village, because this was where important meetings, were held. Why Tiko abrogated his chiefly responsibilities to his college-educated and not full-blooded Fijian sister-in-law was a fascinating question?

The itching and an earache kept me awake. Earlier in the day while wading through the stream I had stepped into a low spot and water got into my ears, dirty water that cows had been standing in. Lania's words echoed in my brain like the beat of a pounding lalo drum: *"I am grateful you are here now and not Beni."* Something like that. No, that was wrong. She never used his name, just said that he wouldn't come here now because I was now reporting on all the farms. We were not even talking about *bulamacows*. What the devil were we talking about? Babies! Yes, we were talking about babies and that there were two without a father and that this had never happened before in her village. Yes indeed, *her* village.

In this country it is the unspoken words that are the truths and the facts. A woman chief without lineage, a self-proclaimed leader in this country, would have to reign without title or ceremony, but it would never stop a woman like Lania from making difficult decisions. I never wanted to cross this lady's path again. I felt used. On the next farm visit I would leave my *bure* at first light, hit the path at a brisk pace to get here, hurry through the reports, and leave the same day. I would not even stay for a cup of tea.

I lay awake a very long time. I knew with a certainty that Lania meant that both babies came from one man—Beni. Mercy! I really did not intend to get involved in Beni's love life. What will this "master of deceit" do when he learns I gave a "no sex lecture" in his private harem? By jungle grapevine he would know within days. I finally fell asleep mumbling, "But I am only a *bulamacow* lady, that's all, only one American *bulamacow* lady with a sick earache."

In the morning on the other side of my curtain I heard Gowena getting breakfast ready. Pulling back the curtain, I found a steaming cup of tea on a cloth spread on the *imbe*. Gowena held out a plate of papaw and a pancake to me. Her smile was just as cheerful as ever and her morning *sulu* as dazzling as yesterday's.

"Good morning, Gowena; that looks good. Are we eating without Tiko?"

"Tiko still sleeps. He has spells of fever and weariness. It always passes in a few days. We eat without him. Here is milk for your tea."

Milk for my tea. Dear God! Did I have milk with my tea last night? I shook my head. "No milk, thank you."

"Gowena, I don't have time to speak to the women in Sote; I must get back. Please remind all the women that they must boil all the milk they drink. Always. Don't forget. All milk."

Try as I might, I couldn't remember if I had drunk milk last night, one of my worst nights in Fiji.

I waded across the stream and changed into dry clothes on the other side. Looking back to Sote, I saw the same pretty, clean village I had viewed the day before. Was it only a lovely illusion? A village bathed in the morning sun, encircled by a slow-moving rippling stream, trees swaying gently in a tropical breeze, and I couldn't wait to get away from it. I never wanted to return. If Gauguin had come here, Lania would have made his stay a torment in his memory and he would have gotten the disease Brucellosis, just as debilitating as the one he died of in Tahiti but without the pleasures, the magic that had inspired his glorious art.

10
Cultural Conundrum?

On my way to the farm nearest to my *bure* I walked up a steep hill, and without warning my legs and knees trembled uncontrollably. I sat down to rest. This had never happened before, and I was frightened. The walk to Orisi's farm was a short one. Six months ago this site visit had been a walk up a garden path. My legs shaky, I returned to my *bure*.

My jeans draped loosely over my hips, but without a mirror or a scale I had no idea how much weight I had lost. The earlier intermittent sore throat and earache had taken up permanent residence. Maria had picked juicy, thick green leaves somewhere in the bush and squeezed their liquid into both ears and told me to lie quiet until I could feel it draining deep inside. After she had done this several times the earache didn't get worse but didn't get better, either. My bottle of aspirin laced with codeine, which I bought over the counter in Suva, eventually did little to ease the pain.

I would slow down a little. Lately, nothing had tasted good. I would have to make myself eat cassava, *dalo*, and an occasional tin of fish. To save energy hiking into my local HQ to get my mail I would give busfare to one of Maria's children to play postman for me. He or she would enjoy visiting their cousins in the village on the way back.

Suni and Beni gave me no support whatsoever, and since my last visit to Sote I had lived with a constant uneasiness. Perhaps that was my problem. Because of Lania in the village of Sote, Beni would know that his trysts in her village were no longer a secret. By jungle grapevine the news of his philandering and my advice for "no sex" would reach him and possibly his pretty young wife. Now Beni had one more reason to wish me gone. He was only comfortable operating in the shadows. I viewed Beni's acts as those of dominance, a game of power.

I met with Suni at least once a month; he always greeted me with the same calm poker face, enigmatic under all conditions, giving no indication of his assent or dissent. If he studied my reports, he knew of the mysteriously appearing cattle on most of the farms, with cattle numbers substantially higher than noted on earlier reports handed in by Beni. Only the farms where Lania's village lay had produced an accurate head count of cattle. And that was the village with an increasing head count of fatherless babies. Did Tiko refuse Beni's cattle grazing on his farm? I was now convinced Beni found vengeance ever so sweet in paradise Sote.

The last site visit of the month was on a farm near the main road. This was a most unusual farm because a young Indian held a ninety-nine-year lease on Fijian land. Indians traditionally raised only goats, the only meat they ate; for this farmer to raise cattle was unusual. He was included by the lending bank as part of the cattle scheme. After finishing the Indian's farm report I planned to get a bus to the local agricultural station, wait for Suni to initial all the reports, and then have lunch. Ten days without eating meat was long enough.

Confoundedly, I counted no fewer then one dozen very thin, almost emaciated young calves, all of them from a dairy breed and all of them approximately the same age. None of the Indian's cows could be their mothers, and also none of the calves were nursing. They needed to be bottle-fed on formula, standard practice when calves are removed from dairy cows. Instead, the calves were trying to eat what they could find in the sparse bush and grass near the road. Where did they come from? One calf standing in the searing noonday sun, weak and unsteady on its feet, was too sick to eat. I took the calf's temperature and found it to be 104.5 degrees; the calf had a dry crusting nose and was seriously dehydrated.

The young Indian farmer was taciturn, even rude, and refused to give any information as to where the calves came from or if they had been tested for TB. To all my questions he answered with a movement of his head or a shrug of his shoulders. He responded to me with the unspoken words, *Women do not question me; this isn't any of your business. Do not question me further. There is nothing wrong with my calves.*

I saw his wife, thin as a rail, wearing a dirty sari, standing in the doorway of a tin-covered concrete house. The only Indian woman in a Fijian village, she must be sick with loneliness.

I found no tattoo in the sick calf's ear, indicating it had been tested for TB. By the looks of all of the calves they could have been infected and might have been born to tubercular dairy cows now giving contaminated milk.

I knew these calves had not been on the farm a month ago. Surely a livestock officer would not sanction the movement of sick calves to a farm. What sort of a dairyman would sell diseased calves? I promptly left this sorry farm without speaking to the Indian further.

I sat on the bench waiting for my bus to Suni's office and arranged my reports in proper order. With this last report on the Indian farm I found approximately one hundred cows and calves without any previous written history of their existence. I had laboriously gone through all bank records in the city. Where did they come from and where did the money come from to buy them? All these facts and I had absolutely no idea what to do with them.

Mysteriously disappearing cattle was an easy puzzle. Those would be the ones sacrificed for marriage feasts or funeral ceremonies. I reported several cows had fallen down hills and broken their legs. This usually occurred twenty-four hours before a scheduled feast. Never did I expect to find so many cattle. And so many sick cows and calves surely must be infecting their owners.

Fijians' and Indians' hatred and intolerance for each other were legendary. How was it possible for a lone Indian to exist side by side with a hundred Fijians? This Indian never attended the many cattle scheme meetings, as no Indian was welcome in Chief Siti's *bure*. Where did he, a poor Indian, get the money? And in the past month?

Schemes were going bankrupt. Disease and poor management took its toll on $125,000 invested in each scheme with World Bank money. My twenty-one-farm scheme appeared to be unique. Sick but unique. With all its disease and poor pasture, my scheme showed up with a respectable increase in cattle. I was obsessed with an eerie feeling of the truth being hidden?

I was reconciled to Beni never having sent my earlier reports to HQ in the city, only stuffing them in the local agricultural station files, where our bosses in Suva never saw them. He was the one breaking procedure and protocol. He was the one hiding facts from Suva HQ. And why? Angrily I asked myself if he understood the American expression "You wanna play hardball—OK, let's play"?

"Suni, where do you suppose all those sick calves came from on the Indian's farm?"

His eyes remained on his papers on the desk. "Ask Beni."

"Good idea. Where is he? We can ask him now."

"Cannot be done today. He's not in. He came in this morning and took the station rifle out of the safe and left."

"But I was told no one in Fiji had a license to carry a gun. Not even the police on the streets of Suva carry guns."

"True, quite true. Only livestock officers may possess a license for a gun."

"In God's name, what for?"

"Renegade wild cattle. Sometimes wild dog packs. Sometimes even a wild boar too near a village."

"*Today* he has a gun. What happened today?"

"A wild bull. One of the farmers on another scheme up north was charged by a bull that has been roaming through the bush for a long time. It is not a good breeding bull but a very dangerous animal."

"Beni will kill him?"

"We certainly hope so. The farmer tried to kill the bull with his machete but never got a chance to even draw blood. The farmer has been laid up for several weeks, very lucky to be alive."

"Do you expect Beni back today? I could wait."

"Probably not for several days. He might have to hunt in the hills for the bull."

"There are so many questions . . ." My words trailed off as I waited for a response from Suni. "Suni, please take a good look at the report on the Indian's farm. I just came from there."

He turned back to my reports and initialed them with only casual glances at them. Was this bureaucrat merely following protocol? Was it laziness? Was he ignorant of contagious diseases and didn't want to know where almost one hundred additional head of cattle came from? What was going on here?

I stood in front of Suni's desk, watching him as he initialed the papers. I studied his face. I could never read this man. After six months with several half-day meetings and a couple of all-day conferences at HQ in the city this man was still a blank sheet of paper to me.

He raised his head and looked me full in my face, his expression impassive and pointedly bored. "Anything else, Barbara? If not, my mother is making an early lunch for me, and the local chief of police has been invited."

Ah, yes! The local police chief, the 275-pound black giant who had visited me during my first month in residence in my little *bure*. When he entered my *bure* I suddenly became claustrophobic. The only words I heard during our tea ceremony was, "Do you share your marijuana with friends?" This interchange many months ago between a newly arrived American and the local police chief was not something I wanted to dwell upon, and I had promptly filed it away in my memory as one more irrelevant cultural conundrum.

I remained standing in front of Suni's desk, my head definitely higher than his. No doubt he understood my growing anger and frustration. Whatever was wrong with Beni was also wrong with Suni. Someone was playing a game on my scheme, and until I found out by whose game rules I would hold my tongue. It was time to evolve my own rules of protocol.

Slowly slinging my knapsack over my shoulder, I politely, if glumly, said good-bye to Suni and walked to the bus stop outside his office. I did not feel well enough for the grueling half-day bus trip into Suva. But if I went back to the bush this afternoon I would only have to come back into town in a few days to catch a bus to Suva HQ to deliver my reports. It would save many hours and miles of walking back and forth on the bush path if I immediately went to Suva. I had on an old skirt and blouse. They would have to do.

A government Jeep drove past me, driven by the town's police chief. He parked in front of Suni's office and went in. It was only natural that the two most important government officials in this small town would be friends. I never was able to figure out why this policeman wanted me to share marijuana with him, a drug I had never tried or possessed. I got on the bus, which did not take me home but into Suva and the next level of bureaucracy. A half-day's trip on a dusty, spine-crunching bus could not be avoided. I also needed more aspirin and codeine.

* * *

In division HQ Richard was out for the entire day, leaving the next higher level Chief Veterinary Officer, Dr. Stevens, for me to see. Stevens, from the United Kingdom, greeted me with a forced smile and a firm handshake. He was a tall, muscular man with unusually broad shoulders and massive forearms. I had been told earlier that he also had a cattle farm. He had the manner of a man who was comfortable giving orders and confident they would be carried out.

"Barbara, come in and have a seat, please. You're late with your reports again, I see."

"Mostly I take a bus in when I can. Here they are, Dr. Stevens. Late, yes, but *far more complete* than previous ones."

I raised my eyebrows and emphasized the "far more complete." Judging by his strong accent, he was born in

Ireland. He was always rigidly correct, even around white men. Dr. Stevens was a sharp-faced, dark-haired man who expected, possibly even demanded, I prove to him I could do my work as well as a man.

"I keep hoping Beni in his government vehicle will bring my reports to you. But so far no luck. Haven't seen him in months. I don't look forward to these rattling all-day bus rides into your city."

He looked at me sideways but said nothing. This was ground we had covered before. The question of why Beni in his government vehicle never offered to help always hung silently in the air between all of us.

An Indian office boy brought two cups of hot tea, and I tried to relax in the stifling heat of Stevens's office. The metal roof conducted scorching heat from the sun, the concrete-block walls were still hot from yesterday, and there was no ventilation. The electric fan was broken. My ankles itched mightily, and I soon found they were speckled with biting fleas. In my bamboo *bure* I was never this uncomfortable, nor did I have fleas biting me. Probably the rats kept them fed.

"Dr. Stevens, we need to test for TB and Brucellosis as soon as possible. Several farms that are, thank God, remote and away from other herds have produced no calves. The farmers won't answer my questions on premature births."

"How remote?"

"Sote, a village on the Rewa River."

"We have an outboard motorboat to bring the blood samples back to the lab. Better than tramping for hours through the bush. Richard and I will set it up."

"Dr. Stevens, after you've looked over my reports I would appreciate your advice. Frankly, I don't have the authority to take the necessary steps. It's the last report on the Indian farmer that is most troubling."

"The Indian farmer?"

I opened the file and placed it before him.

"I see what you mean."

He nodded absentmindedly but remained silent while scanning a few other reports. I reopened the discussion on disease control in the hope of encouraging a conversation, but he was preoccupied. When he finally turned his face toward me, it was cold and bleak. I asked for approved designs in building races, corrals to confine cattle for testing. Listlessly he fingered foot-high stacks of folders on his desk and found what he was looking for. He offered me simple blueprints for constructing corrals.

"We have used these designs for our dairy herds. The farmers can build them without cost from bamboo."

"When will you be able to send your staff from the labs to help with the testing?"

"In a month or two at best."

"So long?"

"Barbara, your scheme isn't the only one with problems."

It was now or never. I stood up very slowly, walked behind my chair, grasped the back, and took a very deep breath. I kept my voice low. The door was open to the larger room, with a dozen Indians working at their desks.

"Dr. Stevens, if you have other cattle operations with more problem than mine you might as well remove all your livestock officers, slaughter all the cattle, and begin anew. The need for testing is not the only issue here. If you study my reports you will see that close to one hundred calves and cows have no record of having been purchased."

Dr. Stevens' eyes suddenly blazed with fury, and he shouted, "Barbara, you go too far."

The heat level in Stevens's office, for me, had reached danger levels. I was dizzy and nauseous. I was not going back into the bush without help from Stevens or another superior.

"Stevens, we should have had this conversation months ago. I'm staying right here in Suva until you and Richard come to a decision. A decision on reducing what we call in the States cattle units. We're in the dry season. We're going to see disease and deaths due to malnutrition."

Stevens finally stood up, reached for my hand, and shook it firmly and long. He was still angry, but he had himself under control. He studied my face.

"Next month, Barbara, when you bring in the next reports. Next month."

"You must understand I can't wait. I'll telephone you in an hour. Before I go back I must have a decision."

In a voice loud enough to be heard in the outer office he said, "Enough, Barbara," and waved me out.

Had I made an enemy? Stevens's anger had triggered a childhood memory. My lovable grandpa advised me that I was expertly talented in my not so gentle art of making enemies. Grandpa's eyesight was poor and I had seen a storekeeper cheat him when returning change. I called the man just that to his face. Grandpa said I needed a lesson in diplomacy and told me to apologize. I refused. He never took me shopping again.

I left HQ and walked into a scorching late-afternoon city heat. The black macadam under my sandaled feet sent sickening waves of foul-smelling chemical fumes toward my face. I felt an uncommon weariness and thought it must be because I had forgotten to eat lunch. My throat felt as if a noose had been tightened around it. It was painful to swallow.

Across the street in front of the bus station a mass of commuters, tired and irritated after a long day working in this dirty city, pushed their way onto rows of buses. The air was gray and acrid from the exhaust pipes of diesel engines. Perhaps after a meal. Perhaps then I could again board one of those smelly machines for the long trip home. But only perhaps. I suddenly thought of a lovely treat that was going to be hard to resist. A delightful way to spend the next hour or so before telephoning Stevens for his answer.

11
Grand Pacific Hotel

In one of the tourist brochures I had seen a color photo of an antebellum nineteenth-century hotel called the Grand Pacific. Now that I was out of the bush I had a sudden craving for something reminiscent of my own culture.

I walked up a wide, curving driveway bordered by spacious luxurious gardens landscaped during the reign of Queen Victoria. At the hotel entrance, between tall white columns, stood a Fijian doorman wearing a uniform of the old empire: black trousers, white jacket with gold epaulets, and a military hat with gold "cabbage" on the visor. He stood at attention and greeted me with a "Good afternoon, madam."

The lobby of the famous Grand Pacific Hotel generously holds hundreds of people sitting or standing. This was an opulence described in romantic nineteenth-century novels and used in multimillion-dollar movies. The elegant white lobby was sparsely furnished with luxurious upholstered bamboo armchairs clustered around plate glass cocktail tables. There were no guests either in the lobby or sitting at a long glossy and waxed mahogany bar nestled against the far wall. Here was the quiet elegance of a century of colonial extravagance in Suva, only a half-day's bus trip from my *bure* in the bush. I needed to be imbued with, and to indulge, if only for a night, in a world I had left behind.

I decided to spend the night. Registering at the desk, I showed my civil servant ID, which entitled me to a 10 percent discount, to a young Fijian in a dark business suit. This slight economy helped to soften a tiny twinge of guilt. Walking through the lobby into a large patio in front of a huge swimming pool, I found a table in the shade with a view of Suva Harbor. I ordered a sandwich, my favorite ham and Swiss, and was served by a Fijian waiter with a starched white napkin over his left arm. I was the only guest on the patio.

In Fijian I asked the waiter, "You have no guests staying at this hotel?"

"When the cruise ship comes, then you will not be alone here. You stay, you will see."

I telephoned Stevens from the hotel desk telephone and learned from one of the Indians that he was gone for the day. I would have to call again in the morning. At any other time and place the news would have infuriated me. In this hotel, still alive with an ambience of a golden age now gone forever, I was ready and willing to escape, for a short time, into its fading enchantment.

That night dinner was a feast with steak that was not horse meat. In my bush town only Australian horse meat was available. The waiters served me wearing spotless white jackets, black tailored *sulu* skirts, black bow ties, clean white gloves, and shoes. They took my order, served, and never made eye contact. The young waiter who silently appeared between courses taking away used dishes hovered nearby, never taking his eyes off my table. Asking him his home village in a dining room lighted with crystal chandeliers and the maître d' watching him would break a rule of etiquette.

On my entering the dining room, the Fijian maître d' examined me from my dusty sandals to travel-worn skirt and blouse and surely questioned my net asset value. He didn't approve of my presence. I agreed with him; the other diners were dressed splendidly for an evening on the town, and they were all white people. When I paid with my American Express card he was clearly surprised.

That night I slept in an immense hotel room furnished with only a single bed, a rickety bureau, and a sagging wicker armchair. The scarcity of furniture only added to the appearance of spaciousness, but unlike resorts on small islands, the electricity was not shut off at bedtime.

The bathroom was as large as my entire bamboo *bure* and the tub large enough for two adults to bathe in at the same time. The bedroom, with its twelve-foot ceiling and white stucco walls, harbored no mouse-sized cockroaches, and the closets hid no rats. I fantasized how this room might have been furnished a hundred years ago for high-ranking British colonial military staff, wealthy traveling businessmen, and their wives dressed in lavish fashionable gowns.

Before going to bed I washed my clothes and hung them under the ceiling fan to dry. If I had no help from Stevens in the morning, maybe I would have to wear them for the third day, too. I made the effort to put Stevens out of my mind for this night.

There was a bedside lamp with an unheard of, in an energy-poor country, a sixty-watt bulb, and I read well past midnight.

In the lobby I had found several crumpled month-old *Wall Street Journals*. Reading *Wall Street Journals*, something I had not done in six months, was a perfect ending to this seesaw day. Dumas's Musketeers didn't give me as much pleasure as these old journals. I was having a party.

Fascinating advertisements: one-year-old Rolls Royce with leather interiors, $200,000; corporate Lear Jet, new avionics, outfitted with double bed, only $2,000,000; Vermont

Bank for sale, assets $1 billion. And all I needed were ten healthy bulls, and testing for disease on 500 or more cattle in poor condition. That night I dreamed of floating on leather cushions over Texas ranches looking for ten Santa Gertrudis or was it ten pure-bred Brahman bulls?

In the morning I telephoned Stevens and was not surprised that he again put me off until later in the day. I would have a few more hours to waste.

I shopped for a bathing suit. The Grand Pacific Hotel had what appeared to be an Olympic-sized pool, and I needed a relaxing swim to soothe my body and growing frustrations.

In a curtained booth in a small shop I tried on bathing suits in front of a full-sized mirror, the first mirror since I left the States. What I saw appeared to be the body of a preteen, not the body of a middle-aged woman with children in college. I grimaced. This was not me. I was not exactly emaciated but certainly had not an ounce of fat. Little wonder this body hadn't needed a bra in months. What for? My chest was now flat, carrying only a prepubescent hint of breasts. My tush was that of a youngster. A body with so little to arouse panting curiosity might as well swim nude in the Grand Pacific Hotel pool. Still, there were all those millions of fat women who would have killed for those legs that went on and on along with that lithe serpentine body. Yes indeed, a serpentine body was preferable over a hippopotamus body anytime. All the swim suits went back on the shop's shelves. Why waste money on a size 8 or 10? I intended to start eating again.

In the late afternoon I was ready for a meeting with Stevens. The Grand Pacific Hotel doorman stepped out in the driveway and blew his whistle toward a taxi parked in the shade of a large tree. The doorman opened the car door for me and told the driver to take me to the regional office of the Ministry of Agriculture. I made myself comfortable in an older-model red Buick in immaculate condition. It appeared to have been newly painted. The driver's faded photo on the license showed a dark-skinned man, probably Indian. His name was J. B. Lal. The name could be either Indian or Fijian, although Lal is more commonly an Indian name. I had never seen a Fijian taxi driver in this country. They cared little for machinery and stayed away from stressful jobs. Also, for them getting several thousand dollars together to buy a car was inconceivable. Did he look familiar to me?

In English I asked, "Driver, I think we've met before, haven't we?"

Silently he shook his head in a "no."

When I entered the cab there was a new-looking white pith helmet on the front seat, a hat no one in Fiji wore anymore; it was a symbol of the old British empire colonialists. Had someone left it behind? No one would wear a pith helmet in this newly independent country. Well, almost no one. I had seen one elderly Brit in a pith helmet wearing a white linen suit with white suede shoes, carrying an ivory-handled walking stick and occasionally stroking his handlebar waxed mustache. He could be seen striding down Suva streets oblivious to the stares and snide remarks or possibly just pretending to be unaware.

"Stevens, thank you for seeing me again. Isn't it a lot too hot in this office? Why don't you get your fans fixed?"

"When we turn on fans the fuses blow. I prefer to see what I'm reading with that one overhead lightbulb."

"Bamboo *bures* are really sensible in the tropics, aren't they?"

"Unless you need privacy."

"What for?" I responded.

His eyes lingered quizzically on my auburn hair, and his eyes scanned my body. Nothing he was examining could possibly incite in him any prurient thoughts, but he still had the capacity to unsettle me. I thought he might very well be the sort of man so secure in his virile masculinity that he believed he could have any woman he chose.

He wouldn't let the topic die a natural death: "Don't need privacy? We all need a little from time to time, don't you think?"

He moved slowly away from his desk and walked over to a hand-drawn map on the wall of his office. It was the map of my eggplant-shaped cattle scheme. Why had I not seen this wall-sized map in Stevens's office yesterday? Or had someone gone to a great deal of trouble drawing it since yesterday? All the walking paths, streams, the large Rewa River at the extreme north boundary, and the main road on the south boundary—nothing had been left to the imagination. Every one of the twenty-one farms was delineated. A red circle in the center toward the north positioned my own *bure*. All the hills were given elevations in detail, and there were many. It occured to me that these elevations should be used to determine where timber might or may not be cut to prevent erosion.

"I'm impressed, Stevens."

"My assistant vet officer, Richard, made it. When you ask for help with sick animals it makes sense to know if we have to hike in or use the boat with an outboard motor. Or in an emergency when a livestock officer has an accident we can fly a helicopter in."

"In an emergency even a marathon runner couldn't get to a phone in under two hours to call for help. The victim's day is ruined by the time help comes."

"Quite right, Barbara, quite right."

"Stevens, on this map you can see where the cattle are, or rather should be, unless they wander."

In a flat, measured voice he said, "And possibly also where they should not be."

Thank the Lord! Stevens had read the reports, and finally someone understood the problem. I didn't need to refer to my reports; my brain was etched with the memory of each farm. With a red pencil I marked every farm with a small x identifying mysteriously appearing cattle. Nonchalantly Stevens watched. I also knew the number of excess cattle on each farm. In my relief at not having to get confrontational with a superior I worked with an intensity that was downright fun. Stevens sat down at his desk, lit a cigarette, and watched the map come alive with red x's and red and blue double-digit cattle units. The blue numbers indicated cattle bought with bank loans. The red numbers indicated the mysteriously appearing cattle.

I stepped away from the wall and waited.

"There is a pattern," Stevens murmured.

"Yes?" I bit my tongue in order not to say any more. If he saw it, my job would be easier.

Stevens mused, "The red x's begin near the town road and move upward into the hills, but there are none near the river. Practically contiguous. With fencing the way it is, it looks like one large herd."

"You're right. No red x's up north, and little wonder," I said.

Stevens's face was now grim, and he said sharply. "Quite."

"Whom do these extra cattle belong to, Stevens?"

"You tell me. You live up there."

"Someone has thousands of dollars to buy beef cattle, and none of it is coming from any bank loan."

"Quite!"

This man's limited vocabulary was beginning to annoy me.

"Stevens, some of these cattle are very sick. You know that farmers get TB; they get Brucellosis. Some cattle are grade three, hardly worth walking out to be trucked to the abattoirs."

Stevens picked up my reports, dropped them with a thud on his desk, and without looking at me said flatly, "I don't doubt you one moment."

The heat in Stevens's concrete office with its sizzling tin roof made me sick.

"Do you agree you need to make decisions?" I asked.

Stevens answered by slowly and methodically leaning back in his swivel chair, placing one sandaled foot on top of his desk and then the other. He lit a cigarette and with an abstracted look in his eyes stared at the map. He was too slow in answering. What was going on inside that closed face of his? Maybe he was wondering where he would have dinner later and with whom. I knew Richard had a British wife and children, but I knew nothing about Stevens. I waited, leaning against the map on the wall.

"Barbara, your job description as livestock officer places management in your and Beni's hands. That is why you were assigned to this job."

There it was. Back in my little bamboo *bure* in the bush. I stood in front of him, spread my hands flat on his desk, leaned toward him, and looked steadily into his narrowing brown eyes. In his sitting position his head was lower than mine. In a village setting, my head higher than his was an act of aggression. Here in the city it meant nothing to him. Angrily I wondered if this country's schizophrenic culture would eventually drive me over the edge.

"You know damn well my colleague has avoided all meetings with me."

"Quite!"

"I don't have the authority to remove almost one hundred cattle units."

"You are right, Barbara, you do not. As soon as we can, Richard and I will begin TB testing and blood sampling."

"Stevens, will it be one, two, or three months?"

My hands twitched. I was close to picking up twenty-one reports to throw at him. It was too close. I turned my back on him and gave the wall map one more long examination.

The isolated village where Principal Lania lived had no red x's and no red numbers. Didn't Stevens see that as an interesting fact? Would Stevens care that Beni left no cattle but did leave his engraved calling card with a fifteen-year-old girl and a woman whose husband was in the army?

Would Stevens care that money given by farmers to Beni to carry to the bank went into his own pocket?

With Stevens's last contemptuous "quite" I was convinced that he didn't give a damn. Neither would Suni. Richard was an unknown quantity.

The map began to weave dizzily. With my back still to Stevens, without a farewell, without the wave of a hand, I left. In the bush I would have been shunned for this impolite behavior. Here in a white man's office it was no more than a ladylike snub, a mild form of contempt toward a superior. How would Stevens respond to my announcement that his boss, Thomas Mitchell, might be interested in hearing me out? Would Stevens again respond with his knifelike "quite"? I intended to ponder this alternative if Richard also was no help.

12
The Hungarian and the U.S. Embassy Lady

The Indian taxi driver dropped me off at my hotel. He was the same Indian who had earlier driven me to HQ, but now he was not driving the red Buick. When he continued around the circular drive I saw him stop next to the Buick taxi parked under a tree. The driver in the Buick took off his white pith helmet and leaned out the window, and I saw the distinctive frizzy black Fijian hair. The two men spoke at length for several minutes and laughed together before the Indian driver moved out into the traffic. They were friends. This was interesting. Even in the cities these two races rarely communicated in any other than a strictly business setting.

    A light misty rain shrouded the evening sky, and I needed to mail a personal letter I'd left in my hotel room. In Fiji all mail is opened by anyone curious enough to wonder what is inside; this was commonplace and until today I had no secrets in my life. This letter was different. If it was read by a local troublemaker my life might become increasingly chaotic. The information was sensitive, personal to my family in the States, outlining current problems in my work. Sometimes when I was writing to my family, living in an entirely different culture it helped me to see more clearly how to proceed. Problems were soon perceived within a refreshingly new paradigm.

Working within this culture, I was wearing a straitjacket; I needed a new perspective. I didn't have as much time as I would have liked because physically I was rundown. I tried not to think about how long I could keep up the pace needed for this job. In fact, I had wasted months while staying inside cultural paradigms. In my letter I let it all out, frustrations, anger, and my suspicions of fraud, embezzlement, and possibly coercion.

In my room in the bottom of my knapsack I found my black nylon raincoat, always with me in a region with a 200-inch rainfall a year, and walked down to the lobby. When the doorman told me the first maildrop box was more than a mile toward town I changed my mind. Tomorrow would be soon enough.

The dining room wasn't open, but the bar was. I draped my raincoat over the back of my barstool and asked the barman to make a Scotch on the rocks with a splash of seltzer. A small group of people sitting close by sipping drinks were the only other guests.

In Fijian I asked the bartender, "Where is your village? Have you worked at this hotel a long time?"

"Many years, Miss Barbara. My home village is on Lau Island. I get very homesick all the time. I go home when I can. Please excuse me now; I have to take these drinks to my other guests."

The barman returned and said, "Miss Barbara, the lady in the red dress said it would be her pleasure to buy you a drink. She also invites you to join her and friends. If you like, let me carry your drink."

I glanced over my shoulder and saw three guests, all Caucasian, relaxing in wicker armchairs. An elegant slender lady in a red silk dress smiled and motioned to me. She was middle-aged and attractive, her blond hair groomed and swept back into a French twist. She held out her hand.

"I'm Marian Boyle; I'm with the American Embassy here in Suva. These are my friends Mr. and Mrs. Farkas. Please come and join us."

The Farkas couple were both dressed in formal white evening clothes. Mrs. Farkas had draped her short, fat body in a silk fabric decorated with white sequins. Her hair platinum blond, the lady glowed and shimmered.

She said, "I heard you speak Fijian to the barman, and so fluently, my dear. You must work here."

White-haired Mr. Farkas, a square-framed man, stood up and bowed toward me. His heels came together, he took my hand, and I felt his fingers linger around my wrist. I couldn't identify his accent. His dark eyes sparkled, and his wide smile appeared as quickly as it also left his face. A composed but pleasant face, I thought.

"By all means," he said, "come sit with us; we can't have you sitting alone. We watched you come down the stairs and wondered who you were as soon as we heard you speak Fijian."

Marian explained, "You see, all of us have been here for several years and none of us have bothered to learn the language. All the locals we do business with speak the King's English."

"Where I work it helps to speak and understand a little of the local language. All of you live here in Suva?"

"My wife and I have for over ten years," Mr. Farkas answered. "One gets used to the country. My wife has all the help she wants. Several Fijian housegirls and a cook we've trained fairly well. And there is always the Suva Yacht club for special celebrations. How about you? Are you alone here?"

I always avoided "alone" questions. Would a lady sit at a bar alone if she was not?

"I'm livestock officer on one of the cattle schemes in the hills."

Marian said, "Of course, Barbara; we meet at last. At the embassy I saw your passport and also your résumé. I'm quite impressed with your qualifications. When you came down the stairs I was almost sure it was you. We might as well have dinner together tonight. The Farkases are headed out to a party."

Mrs. Farkas, adjusted her iridiscent white silk dress over her chubby knees. Her accent was similar to her husband's.

"I wish we could visit with you longer, but we can't be late for this dinner party. You know how touchy these Indians are. We're going to the home of the president of the bank my husband deals with. If one declines a dinner invitation they think you are pro-Fijian and anti-Indian. The animosity between the two cultures is really such a nuisance. I don't know how my husband manages to work so smoothly with all of them."

"This friction between the two races has been going on since the turn of the century, when the British brought indentured Indians here. Isn't it time for them to bury their differences?" I asked.

Mr. Farkas, his voice lowered, said, "Actually, my dear, hostilities are building. Some Indians in my business feel they lived better under British rule."

Marian offered no comment to Mr. Farkas's remark. "Barbara," she asked. "How do you like working with the Fijian farmers? You're rather isolated up there. I understand if an angry cow catches you unaware we must be ever ready to airlift you out with a military helicopter."

"You're right about the cattle. Wild and obstreperous, they consider us the enemy. Back home we make pets of our breeding cattle, but thank goodness the farmers are more tractable than their herds."

"Of course, my dear," Farkas said, "you must be working under Stevens. Handsome fellow. Born and raised in Ireland. He comes to the Suva Yacht Club now and then. But mostly we find he's a loner."

Mrs. Farkas responded with a mouselike squeak and ended with a sound closely related to a soprano "harrumph."

"You have to remember, my dear," Mr. Farkas said, "Stevens knows his business. How many professional men are there who would want to work at this job? All that mud and disease and insects. Not many. He's probably also one of the best vets in this country. Maybe the very best."

He glanced uneasily at me and quickly looked away.

"Yes, dear, I know he is a good vet, but if he's that good what is he doing in this country? He could make three times the money working for the ministry in Australia or New Zealand."

Mr. Farkas flashed a smile at Marian and said, "I think the old boy likes the climate. Let it alone, my dear; just let it alone."

Mrs. Farkas tilted her chin and said defiantly, "It most certainly is not the climate. It's that Indian woman. We all know that."

"Malaysian, my dear, Malaysian, and no, they don't all look alike," said Mr. Farkas. "She is a very cultured lady. Stevens brought her to the Suva Yacht Club once, I understand her husband was a Malaysian general and got into political trouble with the Communists."

"Hm! She probably pushed her husband off a balcony of a tall building in Singapore, just like Stevens did to his wife in Ireland. Those two have more in common than the bed beneath them. Neither one of them has a country to go home to."

This bit of news was greeted with as much enthusiasm as if Mrs. Farkas had given a benign weather report. Marian casually placed a cigarette in her gilt-edged holder, and Mr. Farkas concentrated on spearing his olive out of his martini glass with a toothpick. Mr. Farkas and Marian were not embarrassed. If anything, they appeared a bit bored by the subject of Stevens and his Malaysian lady. Mr. Farkas mumbled something about being late for the bank president's dinner and solicitously helped his wife out of her chair. He bowed deeply to Marian and me. Crossing the enormous lobby, the couple in white moved slowly out into the night within their own silver cloud.

"Lumber. That is why Farkas lives here." said Marian. "First-grade hardwood, trees in such large quantity that the third-generation owner of a Swedish furniture company is thinking of moving to Fiji. The world is hungry for the fine-grained hardwood that can still be found in the hills and mountains of Fiji."

"Farkas buys and sells timber?"

"Yes. He's done very well for himself. More to the point, he employs one of the largest private workforces of Fijians and Indians. This economy depends on men like Farkas."

"How does he juggle the hatred between the two races working under one roof?"

"He has a very big roof, and he's a very savvy fellow. I'm glad you met him. He knows how to avoid dissension and keeps fights from breaking out. He understands the concept of the invisible territorial boundary. A most subtle and diplomatic man."

"He has two feuding races working under one roof without stress?"

"Without stress?" Marian laughed. "There is always stress. What Farkas does is give both races incentives. Bonuses for submission to his will and instant pink slips to the revolutionary. He keeps the men on a short and tight leash."

"The formula of a pragmatist and a benign dictator. Does it really work?"

"For many years. Farkas is a man who sees the many-layered elements in this country and knows how to use and profit from them. The Indians are office staff, and the workers in the lumber mill are only Fijian. Even afternoon tea is prepared on separate hot plates and served in segregated color-coded cups. A Fijian prepares tea for his men and an Indian for his."

"We have Indian loggers on our scheme," I said. "We had a serious boundary dispute over one top-dollar hardwood tree Indian loggers felled. I think they intentionally cut a tree they weren't supposed to."

Marian shrugged her shoulders and commented, "We indulge in wishful thinking when we believe Indians act with the well-being of Fiji as their primary motive. Maybe the tree on the farmer's fenceline was cut by mistake and maybe not. Nothing would surprise me. For decades we've negotiated a fragile peace between two races."

"You think the feud between the farmers was programmed by the Indian logger?"

"The Matangali laws of land ownership limit Indians' quest for commercial gain. They want to buy land, not lease it. Do they divide and conquer? Why not?"

"The two Fijian farmers were ready for bloody combat. They weren't playing games. If one of them had been killed, village life would have gotten ugly."

"Sometimes in Fiji to keep the lid on Barbara, we become, let's say, ingenious. I would be the last person to ask how you managed to keep the peace. But is it going to work again the next time?"

"In another year I'll be safely away from your disputes. I'll be home again on the other side of the world. But yes, while I'm here I will do it again."

"During World War II the Allied forces found the Fijians loyal helpmates. They trained our ground fighting troops in jungle warfare. The Indians, on the other hand . . ." Marian shrugged her shoulders. She never forgot why she worked in the U.S. Embassy.

Marian and I went into the dining room and saw we were the only guests. Four waiters stood at attention against the walls. The maître d' glanced once more at my old skirt and blouse. It occurred to me that instead of trying on bathing suits that morning I might have picked up a decent outfit.

After our waiter took our order and left, Marian leaned across the table and in a soft voice said, "You have a freedom to work here and make decisions in way we cannot. We live here. Our jobs depend on working under the restraints of three cultures. Add the growing Chinese population and we have four."

Marian watched our waiter pour fresh coffee from a sterling silver coffeepot. After he left, she went on.

"The face the Fijian turns toward us, the two percent Caucasian community, is not the face he turns toward our larger Indian community."

"And what does this Fijian face really look like?"

"First tell me the color of the eyes asking this question. Blue, black, or brown?"

"So in Fiji, it helps to have a drop of rabbinical blood running in one's blood. The 'he's right and she's right' voice."

"We accommodate all four races. You met Farkas tonight. He listens to many voices every hour of every day and makes a lot of money doing it. You saw him tonight in a white tux going to dinner at the home of the Indian bank president. Tomorrow you might see him in your village sitting cross-legged, wearing a Fiji *sulu* skirt, negotiating timber prices around the *yanqona* bowl."

Marian took her compact out of her purse and carefully applied lipstick before she continued. "Or he might assign that role to a Fijian. Someone he has trained for the job. A Fijian with a strong connection in the village who knows how to cut a deal, who works for a percentage of the profits."

"Does Farkas know what another twenty years of timbering will do to this island nation?"

"Why don't you ask him? I would be interested in his response."

"He believes," I said, "that he has done a good job bringing this country into the world market."

"Most likely."

"Marian, after the near bloodspilling over one tree I had many bad dreams, all dreams of violence. Before the turn of the century there was constant savage warfare always followed by *cannibalistic* feasts. An elder in my village said it was a way of life. Why the savagery?"

"Over territory! And at a time when there was only one race. Now we have four races."

The waiter brought our dinner tab at the exact moment I spoke the word *cannibalistic* with much emphasis. I searched his face for a response and found only a polite and bland indifference. His eyes carefully scrutinized the tablecloth. He was trained not to make eye contact with a superior—a white lady—but I knew he had heard my words and I regretted that.

After dinner Marian and I parted on the front steps of the hotel. We exchanged addresses and made plans for another visit together. The red Buick taxi drove up, and inside I saw the driver wearing a white pith helmet.

On the way to my room I stopped at the bar for the raincoat I had draped over the barstool earlier when I had joined Marian and the Farkases for a drink. It was gone. The barman said he didn't know where it was. He only worked at the bar if there were customers. I was annoyed not because of the cheap missing slicker but because my personal letter was also gone. In my letter I had referred to Beni as the "phantom livestock officer." Had I written his name? I couldn't remember. I had gone into detail about his fathering two babies and the mysterious appearance of calves that dropped from the heavens.

To the barman I said, "It doesn't matter about the raincoat. It's the letter. I don't remember if my letter was in the pocket of my coat or if I left it at the bar or possibly on the cocktail table."

The barman's face relaxed into a broad smile. He said, "*Senga na lenga*, Miss Barbara, *senga na lenga*. The doorman came over for a drink of water, and when he saw your letter he said he would mail it for you. He is at the door now. Why not ask him?"

"Miss Barbara, I saved you walking to the mail drop in the rain. I gave the letter to the taxi driver to mail for you. You know the driver in the red Buick. He said he would be happy to help."

Were taxi drivers as snoopy as villagers in the bush? Surely not this one, a city man who had a lot more interests in life than opening other people's mail. In the bush all my magazines came months late and dog-eared and most of my mail had been clumsily resealed before I received it. I had gotten used to it. But I was uneasy about this letter written only for the eyes of my American family.

I wandered out to the empty patio and walked around the pool. The rain had stopped and the water was surprisingly cool. I was too tired for a swim anyway. There was absolutely nothing I could do about the letter. Nothing. I sat down in one of the chaise longues and watched the lights of an anchored freighter dance on the waters of Suva Harbor. The ship, which I had seen earlier, was rust-stained, a Soviet freighter. The captain saved thousands of dollars a day by berthing in the harbor instead of at the pier. Or was he afraid of Russian seamen jumping ship? The unhappy sailor would not get far. The island isn't big enough or friendly enough to hide the stranger, the "Rusky."

The barman came out of the hotel carrying a silver tray perched on three fingers. He handed me a half-filled glass with gold liquid over ice.

"Compliments of the hotel. Miss Barbara. I am sorry someone took your raincoat. Very sorry."

"*Senga na lenga*, no problem. Do not worry yourself. Be sure to thank the hotel for me; this will help me sleep."

I looked up into his face and knew that his quick glance had only just caught my wink before he turned away.

The Scotch helped me relax in the cooling breezes of a tropical night. If I lived permanently in this country I would turn day into night. The evening caresses while the day's tropical sun punishes and chastises. I stretched out on the chaise longue and mused over Marian, a successful diplomat, a lady elegant and restrained, everything my own mother would have wanted me to be. I remembered the day years ago when I showed Mother a new $10,000 bull in back of my farm truck: a symbol of success in a tough business, owning bull from the most famous pedigreed bloodline in the States. Mother took a quick look and announced. "A fine-looking ox, yes indeed, a mighty fine-looking ox." But that was a long time ago.

After the baffling meeting with an obdurate Stevens, dinner with Marian had been a joy. I would send a little note in the morning thanking her for a lovely evening. Except for her silence when I told her how disappointed I was with Stevens, she had been generous with her ideas.

Stevens? His dead wife buried in Ireland, did he really kill her? A shrewd man. A calculating man. *Persona non grata* in his birth country. A man without a country living with a Malaysian widow woman without a country.

Stevens had said all management decisions were to be mine. Not exactly—he had said "yours and Beni's." So be it.

In the morning I woke to find a letter pushed under the door. It was an invitation for lunch at the Suva Yacht Club with Mr. Farkas. Mrs. Farkas was not mentioned. My wardrobe would not work at a private club designed for the upper-crust colonial empire and the 2 percent elegant white population. Shopping for a dress for one lunch at the Suva Yacht Club would be a waste. I telephoned Farkas and suggested lunch poolside at my hotel, and he agreed. After lunch I would decide whether to head for home or stay one more night. The rest was doing wonders for my chronic weariness.

Farkas stepped out on the patio and coolly surveyed the large lunch crowd. He was again dressed in white—tennis shoes, slacks, and polo shirt—with a cobalt blue silk scarf around his thick, short neck. He marched briskly toward my table not looking left or right.

"Barbara, how lovely; thank you for accepting my invitation."

He bowed and again grasped my hand fully and let his fingers linger around my wrist with a faint tickling sensation. After he sat down he smoothed down his white hair by slowly pressing both hands firmly front to back along the sides of his head. There never was a single silver hair out of place. But there was a tiny black smudge on his chin.

"And please let's not be too formal; call me Laszlo. As you might have guessed, I am Hungarian. I was born in Budapest."

He pronounced his city's name correctly: "Budapescht."

"And your wife is also Hungarian?"

"Yes, she is. There is a reason why she does not have as strong an accent. Before World War II her parents escaped with their children and were given political sanctuary in England. You see, she is descended from the Esterhazy family, the royal family of the Austro-Hungarian Empire."

"She does look quite royal. A very pretty lady. And you, Laszlo! Any royal blood in your veins?"

The flash of his radiant smile never held long. He gave a short, sardonic laugh.

"Thank you for the compliment. I try. My wife expects me to live up to her standards."

"You succeed admirably, Laszlo."

"Thank you. You are very kind. The name Farkas comes from the word *wolf* and in Hungary always denotes working-class. My father owned a vineyard. He expected I, too, would work with the grapes. But it was not to be. The Communists imprisoned him when he refused to leave his land. He died in prison." For an instant Laszlo's hands cut the air, an involuntary show of helpless anger. "Enough about old Laszlo. Now we need to know all about Barbara. But first I promised you lunch."

Laszlo snapped his fingers several times at the waiter coming onto the patio with a tray of drinks for lunch guests. A large cruise ship had arrived in the Suva that morning and released 2,000 tourists into the city. Noisy groups of American tourists had earlier come through all the doors of the hotel and now sat around umbrella tables.

"Laszlo, now I know why you suggested lunch at your private club. My fellow Americans are a bit noisy. Please accept my apology."

Laszlo gave our lunch choices in a staccato rhythm. The waiter never looked up from his pad and pencil while taking the order. He didn't like Laszlo. I also knew he was disappointed that the nice *bulamacow* lady was having lunch with this man. I had lived in the bush long enough to read subtle Fijian signals that said, *I will be polite to you, but you will always be a stranger to me.* I don't know when or how I learned these unseen, nonverbal signals. But I was now in my own white culture and felt an impatience with the waiter. He had no right to approve or disapprove of my lunch companions.

"Barbara, I had planned to show you my yacht at the club. You probably do not have many friends with boats."

"Now I know where you got that tiny spot of oil on your chin. Checking grease fittings on your diesel engines? Here, I will wipe it off for you."

"You are an observant girl, aren't you? You know, you are a bit of a puzzlement to this old Hungarian. In our country the only women who touch cows tend not to have other options. From what Marian tells me, you have credentials for, well—"

"For me the time came for this particular job. I chose it. It did not choose me. Still puzzled?"

"I won't pry, Barbara. I thank my God that I also have choices in life and that I don't have to live in a cold Communist land. Let us drink to Fiji, my adopted home. I intend to do business here until I die. I learned a toast from my father I like very much. It goes something like this: 'May we never meet a friend on the way up the ladder of success.'"

I have always admired "take charge" men who don't make excuses for taking charge. I relaxed in his company. Perhaps he was a little too shrewd, but with his World War II experiences, first with Nazis and later with Communists, he had opted for survival. He was the alpha man, a goal man, a focused man. I admired him. Possibly his murdered father had also been an alpha.

Over coffee Laszlo brought up the business on his mind, which was somewhat of a relief, because without his wife with us there would have been only one other reason for an invitation to lunch.

"Barbara, I've recently bought some damned good lumber off your cattle scheme—in fact, the best on this island this year. It's not as easy finding grade-one hardwoods as it was a few years ago."

"The little I saw logged is virgin timber. Some of it looks like mahogany, but then again, I don't know the trees of this country."

"Only here do we still have virgin trees of top quality. The last shipment to my lumberyard came from your scheme, and this is the quality I'm looking for, the best. I shipped that lumber to Sweden for veneer."

"You run a tight operation, Laszlo. One day the Indian forester came to measure board feet. The next day more Indians came with their team of oxen and pulled the felled trees down to the road to waiting diesel trucks. Usually in this country everything takes weeks and months."

"The Indian forester you met is a good friend of mine. He told me all about the American *bulamacow* lady up in the bush."

"He has an important job," I said. "For the Fijian farmer this may be the only income he'll see this year. The only role I play is making sure the board feet are measured by a licensed forester. My presence is also to remind the farmers that the money should be used to pay off their loans at the bank."

"He's professionally trained. He works for the Ministry of Forests."

"An Indian working for a Fijian boss?"

Laszlo laughed and said, "In this country the Fijian bosses sit behind government desks making policy. If they make good decisions it is by pure accident. It's the men in the field who make all the important decisions."

He lifted his glass, swirled the ice cubes and appeared lost in thought. A moment later he looked intently into my eyes and said, "I said 'men in the field.' Forgive me, Barbara I should have said 'men and women in the field.' "

The muscles in his jaws tightened, and he sat stiffly and leaned toward me. So this was not a simple lunch between two expatriates. He wanted something from me. His on-again, off-again smile made me uncomfortable, so I focused on the Fijian waiter weaving between crowded tables, balancing large trays of drinks. He was working hard, drops of perspiration glistening on his forehead. He would make as much in tips today as his father made in six months growing tapioca and *dalo*. The waiter was polite, but his face was expressionless. He was feeling stressed. When complimented by a loudmouthed American matron, he answered with a mumbled, "Vanaka vaka levu," knowing full well she didn't understand him. What a waste! Halfway around the world and none of these touristing Americans would ever feel the mystery of the shrouded tropical rain forest, the thundering waterfalls, or the tranquillity of hidden villages. What a damn waste. From a floating four-star hotel to another land-based four-star hotel and no one would ever see the magic of this island nation. Laszlo became annoyed at my wandering attention and called me back to him.

"Barbara, the price I pay the farmers on your cattle scheme depends on the quantity and quality of the hardwoods. We have several different-numbered grades based on wood variety and other factors. It can get very complicated."

Casually facing him, I said, "When the chief in my village asked me to be present while the Indian measured your trees, I was truly puzzled. I know nothing about your business, Laszlo, nothing about grading wood."

"My dear Barbara, you know a great deal. You write all the contracts between the Indian loggers and the Fijians."

"Only to prevent conflicts. When expectations are not met arguments result. My grandfather taught me a simple rule in life he called the Three A's: Always Avoid Arguments. Legal instruments serve this intent. On my farms in the States I might have as many as three contracts at any given time with various farmers. In your business you must have a file cabinet with hundreds of timber contracts."

Laszlo leaned back in his chair, his eyes narrowed and his mouth firm. "Sometimes contract law can get in the way of good business, Barbara; surely you must know that."

"These contracts, these simplistic agreements, deal only with the number of board feet measured, with the Indian classifying grades of timber."

Here we go, I thought. Somehow, someway, these simple one-page contracts interfered with Laszlo's profit margin. I really didn't care to know how. I concentrated on looking around the now noisy and heavily drinking cruisers. I needed more time. So did he. He was looking for the correct words to use on me I felt sure would not be in the best interest of my farmers. It might be downright dishonest.

He was unrelenting. "Barbara, before you came we had no written lumber contracts. Beni was the one who was present during the measuring of the felled timber. He was the one who watched the forester fill in the forms for quality and quantity. I place a value on his—shall we say—negotiating skills. That is, of course, negotiating the price I pay the Fijians. I, of course, make it worth his while. Without an ally in this business—"

He was interrupted by a cruise ship's "all aboard" horn sounding three short bursts and the immediate loud and unruly response of a hundred tourists making their way from the patio and through hotel doors.

With my eyes still on the departing crowd I casually asked, "When was the last time you saw Beni?"

"Beni? Today, when he picked me up at the yacht club in his taxi, his pride and joy, his red Buick."

Involuntarily my head turned sharply toward Laszlo and I fought back instant rage. Beni was the owner-driver of that taxi. I wanted to get up and run from Laszlo. Was Laszlo the reason for Beni's absence from the cattle scheme? Or was Laszlo only part of the problem?

"Sweet Jesus! Of course! The red Buick taxi. Of course, oh, my God!"

My intensely personal letter was in Beni's hands, documenting all his chicanery and deceit, lacking only the percentage of profits on timber sales.

"But why do you look so upset, my dear? Everyone knows about him and his taxi. Everyone! It is no secret."

I wanted to scream at Laszlo, "Of course! Everyone but me." I stood up too quickly, and my chair tipped, I put it back in its place, mumbled an "excuse me," and followed the last tourist hurrying through the doors. Behind me I heard Laszlo snap his fingers repeatedly and shrilly call for the waiter.

In my room the maid had laid a fresh hibiscus blossom on my pillow. My heart was pounding. I held the blood red blossom in the palm of my hand and saw the yellow pollen smudge in my sweaty palm. A blossom, always the universal symbol of innocence, no matter which way I turned the flower I would see the blossom as the world saw it. But I saw Farkas last night and I saw Farkas today, and it is the same man with another face. Ironic, that his name in Hungarian spells wolf.

I had never fully looked into Beni's face, but now I knew he had two. No, he had more than two. He had one face he showed to his boss, Suni; one for Marian in the embassy, who tried to warn me; another for Stevens, who can never again go home; another face Beni showed to the Indian; and yes, of course, the name of that Indian taxi driver was J. B. Lal and he was the man who held the license on the red Buick taxi Beni drove and owned, which was bought with money given to Beni by the farmers to bank. Beni embezzled cattle scheme money. Accepting a percentage of Farkas's profits was wrong and timbering the Fijian rain forest was a disaster waiting to happen.

Ah, but I forgot Beni's face as seen in the eyes of the young married and unmarried mothers of his babies in Principal Lania's hidden village. By now how many villagers knew his various faces? Would the traditional *keri keri* and *vasu levu* culture forgive him? And if a man has six faces what will stop him from having more?

The crushed blossom bled red and yellow fluid in my clenched fist, etching tiny streams between my knuckles. I went into the bathroom to wash my hands and looked at myself in the mirror. What face did Farkas, Marian, Stevens, Richard, Suni, Chief Siti, and the Fijians in the villages see when they looked at me? A victim? Was that how they saw me? Someone who came from a wealthy country and was here for their use and manipulation?

I might respond to their games as an hilarious comedy. I, the bungling buffoon, tripping in and out of their lives, bouncing from one cultural component to another, always befuddled, predictably impotent. Was this an all too familiar feeling most of us shared? One of helplessness? Certainly Stevens, a man without a country, felt helpless, Marian, a career diplomat, was vulnerable; it was easy for Principal Lania to manipulate me in trying to protect her teenage girls; and all those inexperienced farmers scratching out a living, did they feel helpless?

Farkas was the only one who had the freedom to choose. Was he damaged by the Nazis and later the communist atrocities in his country? Without any of that would he be acting any differently? No way to know.

The palpable consuming hatred I felt for a man with whom I'd had only one conversation—Beni—was definitely an effective motivator for me to act. I felt a desperate need to act. To what end? Anything to vent this pressure. I must get back to the bush to think. But if I left now, nothing whatsoever was resolved. Worse, Beni was now driving Farkas back to his lumber yard. Now Beni knew his every face was known to me.

I filled the bathroom basin with cold water. To calm down I poured water over my face. I spoke to my reflection in the mirror: "In the morning I leave, but not until I meet with Richard. To hell with Stevens!"

Richard knew I was coming. I found him sitting at his desk reading a newspaper, and he looked tired.

"I should warn you, Barbara, Stevens called me yesterday. There isn't anything I can do to help you. It's your job to make management decisions. I'm the vet. You're the manager."

"That's right, Richard. You're the vet. I'm telling you to TB- and Brucellosis-test all the cattle on the scheme during the next two months. I cannot do that; you can."

"Without races, corrals, that's an impossible job."

"Richard, this is a statement. Not open for discussion. Remember the story you told me about the bats in the *vale lailai*?"

"The teacher went back home."

"I've just experienced my own bats in the *vale lailai*."

Richard put down his paper and rubbed both hands over his face. Was he hoping he could somehow wash me clear out of his life? Was he tempted to accept my resignation? Probably he was considering it. I almost, but not to any viable degree, felt sorry for him. I gave him a few moments to comprehend.

I said, "In one month the races will be built; eight should be enough. Farms sharing boundaries will build races to be used communally, and you can start testing."

"How in blazes do you expect them to finish all this in one month?"

"Otherwise the men won't get the four more bulls they need. I won't let a healthy bull anywhere near this scheme until I've gotten rid of every infected animal."

"Two months?"

"Yes, no longer!"

"Who's going to deliver this wonderful bit of news to twenty-one lazy Fijian farmers?"

"You are, in one week, at a scheme meeting in Chief Siti's *bure*."

"Bloody likely."

"You're the vet. Not me. Disease is your job. For this you need to make plans. A method of keeping the vials of blood from boiling over in the noonday sun before you get them to your labs."

"Barbara, you don't know what you're asking. Those farmers are going to shrug me off. They've done it before."

"You will tell them they will not be selling any more trees until their herds meet your health standards. From this day forward no more timber sales."

"They won't listen to me. And what the hell does timbering have to do with cattle diseases?"

"These men aren't stupid. They want to do what's right for their land. None of them have ever had experience in land use. In just two years the men have seen the damage done by clear cutting. Entire hills are mud slides. Streams from which they got their drinking water have been spoiled. They will listen to you."

"Stevens knows what you're asking?"

"He advised me to go back and manage. As you know, veterinary medicine is your responsibility. Stevens looks like a man who's sick to death of his job. He won't make the hard decisions. Perhaps he wants to spend more time on his own ranch or perhaps with his Malaysian lady. What do you think?"

Richard raised one eyebrow. "So you've been getting out of the bush more and more lately."

"It's been a learning experience, Richard."

"All right, all right. Next week a geologist from Australia is visiting the College of the South Pacific for a series of lectures. He could help by setting up a land use plan for timber cutting based on gradients, elevations, and soil analysis on your scheme. It should really have been done years ago."

"I soil-tested all of Orisi's farm, hills, and valleys. It's a start. The Ministry of Forests should be doing this all over Fiji."

"Right."

"Richard, the farmers will also be more likely to listen to someone like this geologist than to us."

Richard sighed, not happy with our meeting but resigned. He took out his pocket calendar, slowly turned pages, and said, "One week from today at Chief Siti's home I'll bring the *yanqona*. Seems I heard, Barbara, something about you loving the stuff."

"Ah, yes, the bush telephone travels all the way into Suva. You might have warned me about your drug culture. One more bit of news. I'm heading back to the bush tomorrow. I need your hand-written letter on your HQ stationery giving Suni orders to get that rifle out of Beni's hands and back in the safe where it belongs."

"Beni's got a rifle?"

"Yes indeed!"

"Bugger! Who the hell is in charge up there?"

"What exactly does *bugger* mean, Richard?"

"Its something to do with bugs copulating."

Borrowing Steven's favorite word, I exclaimed loudly, "Quite!" and left Richard looking at me with a crooked smile.

Was it perhaps possible that among all the men and women who might have made my job more manageable and chose not to, only Richard had nothing to hide, nothing to lose? Despite my first impression of him many months ago, a closed-faced aristocrat who never gave out any more information than I could drag out of him, Richard in the end was the only superior I had who was not afraid to save the cattle scheme from one more disaster. So what did he have to gain?

13
Home Sweet *Bure*

Two buckets of clean water stood in front of my *bure*. Faithful Ili had guessed I would be coming home tonight. Placing my liter tin of kerosene and knapsack inside, I went to my small vegetable garden to pick a handful of wing beans for supper. A crumpled wad of blue paper lay on the ground under the vines. It was the airmail letter to my family, now torn open, describing in detail all of Beni's activities, the letter the doorman had given the taxi driver, Beni, to mail. I smoothed the wrinkled, damp letter and heard Ili calling out her cheerful greeting to me.

"Ili, did you see anyone come to my *bure* yesterday or today, anyone at all?"

"No, Miss Barbara, I was in school both days. Is something missing?"

Ili's eyes widened and she said, "Do not tell my mother. My mother will scold you. She says when I lose something it is bad luck because it might be found by the *tevoro*, the sorcerer who lives up the path in the hills. And when it is returned to me it is taboo. There will be a black spell on it, and then when I touch it the spell will stick to me."

It was always a temptation to laugh at Ili's view of events she could not understand. This event, however, a letter lost in a luxurious hotel in Suva mysteriously showing up many miles away in the hills and in my vegetable garden, where was the humor in it?

"Ili, your mother is only trying to keep you from losing your books and sweaters and things. Maria doesn't really believe in black spells."

"My mother does and so does my father. I have to go eat my supper now. I'm glad you came home; my mother and father worried about you. Father was going to go looking for you tomorrow."

I felt sorry to have worried Maria and Tomaci. I forgot they might worry, that anyone would worry about me.

If Ili was right, holding the letter I was contaminated with the spirit of the incorrigible Beni. Voodoo and taboo beliefs have fascinated most of us since childhood. At Halloween I always looked forward to creepy sensations listening in the safety of my home to legends about ghosts and the not-quite-dead. This was not the same. This man was close to me, knew more about me than I did about him, and had gone to great lengths to let me know that he was now watching me. With this warning he wanted to frighten me, and he was succeeding.

I lit my Coleman stove and with a pot scooped up water from the bucket to bring to a boil for my next day's drinking water. Supper would be Velveeta cheese and bread and powdered milk.

I heard soft childish giggling going on outside my *bure*, a bit surprising so late in the day. I waited for a knock, but none came. Opening the door, I found a young girl and her slightly older brother grinning up at me. They were the children of Vita, a neighbor who lived only a mile down the path. The boy was hiding something behind his back, and it was obvious he was giddy with a wonderful surprise gift for me.

"Come inside, please. Why are you out so late? Does your mother know where you are?"

"My mother said to bring this to you for your dinner. She says you are too skinny; you must eat more meat."

In my outstretched hands the boy placed the largest, ugliest, fur-covered dead bat I had ever seen. I made every effort not to show revulsion and not to hand it back to him.

"A fruit bat. Mother said cook it in a pot. Very good meat on fruit bat. Good for one meal."

"Your mother eats bat?"

"When we knock bat out of tree with a rock or a stick Mother cooks bats for us. Very good to eat."

I forced myself to stroke the soft brown fur and stretch out the leathery wing between the bat's arm and its body. Fully stretched out, the fruit bat was about a foot wide. The fur-covered head was a fox's head in miniature, actually quite elegant. Could I really skin this creature of the night, cook this tiny body and sinewy arms and legs, and with my teeth pick thin shreds of muscle from its bones? I gave the children a bit of candy, handed them their fruit bat, and told them I had already eaten my supper and sent them back home. The children tried to look disappointed, but they also knew what they were going to have for supper.

I would have to apologize to Vita. She was only trying to return a favor of mine. Tomaci and Maria had held Sunday morning religious service in their *bure* and invited me. It was a simple Methodist service, with Vita's husband officiating as a lay minister. Vita was sitting next to me, but soon she curled up on the floor and I knew she was in pain. She whispered to me that her head was hurting so bad she felt sick. I took her up to my *bure* and gave her two aspirin and told to lie down and sleep. An hour later, when I returned, she was still sleeping soundly. I asked Ili if she had these headaches very often and was told the bitter fact that her husband, the lay minister, was fond of beating her. Vita had sent her children to me with a *sevu sevu*, the present of a fruit bat, to repay me for two aspirin.

I was in bed with the mosquito net tucked in, reading a book, when a soft knock came on my door and Ili's voice announced herself.

"Miss Barbara, my father wants to talk to you."

This was the first time Tomaci had come to my door; he usually sent Ili or one of his young sons. Tomaci spoke only bush dialect and no English at all. Ili was his interpreter tonight.

"My father wants to borrow your hammer and nails and fix your three doors so they cannot be opened from the outside."

Tomaci looked at me, clearly feeling insecure about something. He was holding three pieces of lumber, two feet by one foot, and I wondered where he got them. Milled lumber in the bush is a scarce item, and his *bure* was bamboo and thatch. I watched as he nailed the planks on the outside of my doors.

Ili said, "'Now my father wants you to latch your doors on the inside and he will go outside and try to open them."

I did what he asked, and saw as his machete on the outside slide between the jamb and the door. It was unable to lift the simple wood lever on the inside.

I opened the door and saw Tomaci smile sheepishly at me. He mumbled a, "Vanaka, sa mothe sa mothe," and I watched him and Ili disappear into the night.

First Vita with her unique gift of bat meat, then Maria and Tomaci—my families in the bush were not only worried but also now clearly afraid for me. Their loyalty to the village was sacrosanct; questioning them as to why, would only embarrass all of us. Years ago a rabbi, a friend of mine, explained the concept of negative truths to me. It is always wrong to spread a negative truth about someone even if it is absolutely true. He said the concept was called *lashon hara*. My rabbi friend will be happy to know that if *lashon hara* is the only criterion for being an observant Jew there are many Fijian Jews he doesn't know about.

That night for the first time in my life I lay down to sleep aware of a fear new to me. My two machetes were under the mosquito net, one on either side of me, and I felt a little ridiculous about this and the fact that I had sharpened them with my file until they were sharp as razors. The wick of the small kerosene lamp was turned up as high as possible for maximum light. Would the rats come out for their nightly raid? Only seven more hours of this unsettling black tropical night and there would be Ili, on her way to school, knocking on my door reminding me to get ready for a new day. I practiced my nightly routine of finding one more belly laugh to restore balance to one more worrisome day. How would a French gourmet chef, with only a fruit bat available for the main entrée, prepare such a dish?

14
Lasa

To be goal-oriented in Fiji is to go insane. Expect to go from A to B and back to A, and before you know you find yourself at Z, wondering where you went wrong not to have passed B. I learned too late not only to be suspicious of Fijians and their *keri keri*, giving something without knowing you are giving until it's too late, but also to be suspicious of trusted friends, white, black, or brown. *Keri Keri* is contagious. With time the *keri keri* and a *vasu levu* culture seep insidiously into the psyche of all.

And that is how I met Lasa. The word *Lasa* means "easy, pleasant, and delightful." Gorgeous twenty-year-old Lasa, with her voluptuous body, childlike smile, and skin the color of mocha coffee light on the cream, might have taken her name as her totem. In her village the story told is that even as a youngster she cheerfully, generously acted out every nuance of her mellifluous name. Lasa made up little dances for the *mekes* dances. And this in an environment of wretched poverty.

I met Lasa's family before seeing her. I traveled to her isolated village for a site visit only because I had been promised three or four days of rest and a stay at an adjacent resort close to the most spectacular coral reef in Fiji. My spirits soared. I was told the coral reef and fish were as richly diverse as those in the Great Barrier Reef of Australia.

All I had to do was fly to Vanua Levu, the second-largest island of Fiji, and a government Jeep would whisk me away to a luxurious hotel and later, at a time of my choice, the driver would take me to the village.

"Who requested this site visit? There's an ag station on the island—why me?"

"They're understaffed. The request came from a man of the village."

"Are we talking goats or cows?"

"Who knows? Have a great time. You can borrow snorkel equipment at the hotel. Even the sharks are friendly."

I boarded a twin-engine plane with a dozen other passengers and watched a young Fijian man, finding the flight was overbooked, buckle himself into the copilot's seat.

The Fijian pilot, who looked to be in his midtwenties, boarded, locked the cabin hatch, and without a glance toward the passenger sharing his cockpit, taxied toward the runway. After an engine runup check he turned into the active runway and we were airborne. He leveled out and for the rest of the flight we were in solid cloud cover.

The grinding sound of the plane's flaps being lowered was the first clue that we were approaching Vanua Levu. The view out the cabin window was an impenetrable white-out. The pilot took his visored cap off, opened his window, stuck his head into the dense wet cloud, and looked forward, down, and then aft. He continued to fly the plane with his head outside the cockpit for several minutes. No radar assist, no glide slope indicators, no OMNI ultra-high-frequency radio beams, the pilot was flying a dead-reckoning flight plan. What if the winds aloft were capricious? What if he had forgotten to wind his watch and didn't know how long he had been flying at a designated airspeed? All the other passengers, Fijians, were relaxed and unconcerned.

Miraculously, the clouds dissipated, ocean waves broke on a palm-studded beach, and as I looked over the shoulder of the pilot a short runway surrounded by mangroves appeared before us. The pilot throttled down and made a smooth landing. There were no airport buildings, no attendants visible, and, most important, no government Jeep waiting to chauffeur me to that four-star resort hotel with a world-class coral reef within a short swim.

The pilot stacked baggage beside the plane, pulled a short ladder out of the compartment, climbed up to the top of the plane's cowl, and checked on oil and fuel. Climbing down, he headed toward some thick bushes on the edge of the runway. Without any gas tanks visible, perhaps there were barrels of fuel somewhere in the shade out of the heat of the sun. Wrong again. He reappeared zipping up his shorts. Within minutes he was airborne again and into the clouds.

I waited under a rusting corrugated metal roof for my ride to the hotel. All the other passengers disappeared down a narrow dusty road. I was hot, thirsty, and uneasy with no idea where the hotel was. After a half hour I decided I might as well start up the road as the other passengers had done. Some village must be within walking distance—I hoped not more than a mile or so. Soon an open government Jeep came toward me, leaving a blinding dust plume behind that soon enveloped me within its gritty cloud.

"Miss Barbara?"

"*Io, bula bula.* You're very late; I was getting worried."

"*Senga na lenga*, no problem, Miss Barbara, no problem. I wasn't told until a few minutes ago that I was to pick you up."

"Let's get to the hotel then, I'm tired and—"

"Miss Barbara we are not going to the hotel just yet. I was instructed to take you to the village as soon as you arrived. We leave now."

With one foot inside the Jeep, one on the road, I turned angrily toward the driver. He continued to sit in the Jeep. Even if the site-visit village was only a one-hour drive, I didn't feel up to it. No way.

"Driver, what's your name?"

His voice had a sharp edge. "Waisale, Miss Barbara, Waisale."

"We go to the hotel, Waisale. Tomorrow or the next day we go to the village. Now we go to the hotel."

Waisale made no response except to jerk the gears into low, and soon we were driving fast down a bone-jarring dirt road. Waisale was probably even older than he looked. His face, stern, never changed in its intense concentration on the road before us. He wore an American military hat, visor cracked; whatever insignia had graced it decades ago had been ripped off, leaving the front with a torn opening. As a teenager he might have worked in one of the World War II installations. Just my luck to have a driver who was probably a village chief. Only a chief would be as severe and uncommunicative. He knew I was angry, and he also knew I was at his mercy.

As it was impossible to carry on a conversation over the roar of the Jeep's engine minus a muffler, I sank into a grumpy silence. We had driven almost one hour, passing several villages, before my patience was spent. Surely the hotel was not this far from the only airport on the south coast of Vanua Levu.

"Waisale, where the hell is this hotel? There hasn't been a beach within sight since the airport."

"We go to your village. One hour, maybe more, we'll be there."

"The village? What village?"

"The village I was told to take you to. Its minister is also the chief. He waits for you near his church. No problem. We get there before dark."

"I can't do my job in the dark. There isn't enough time today."

"I come back for you same time tomorrow. No problem."

Waisale, shrewed and tough, had outsmarted me, outmanuvering me and my anger. HQ in Suva, his boss, had given him a job to do, and he did it. I was nothing more than a package to be delivered.

The island of Vanua Levu is only about one hundred miles long and twenty miles wide, and roads are mere dirt tracks. Near the coast schoolchildren walk several miles through mangrove swamps to get to the roads where their public schools are. In the winter, at dusk young children maneuver slime-covered terrain to arrive home for their supper and early bed. Nobody has money for flashlights.

By late afternoon Waisale stopped at a modest wooden Methodist church with only a hint of the original white paint. A tall, slender Fijian man, middle-aged, with deep-set eyes, rose from the church steps, reached into the backseat of the Jeep, lifted out my knapsack, and held it out to me. He was bare-chested and wore only a frayed *sulu* skirt held together by a large safety pin. There wasn't enough fabric left to bunch up the ends and tuck them into his waist. I was introduced to Chief Navitalai, the minister of the church. Usually a church is within sight of the village it serves, but not this one: this sad old house of worship sat on miles of deserted road, not a *bure* or shack visible.

Waisale and the chief never spoke to each other. Waisale made a U-turn and sped off.

I wasn't prepared for the more than one hour of balancing astride slick coconut logs and picking my way through shallow, evil-smelling black water. The chief, barefoot, walked elegantly and lightly ahead of me, only occasionally glancing back at me. I had one nasty ankle-twisting fall in water hiding mangrove roots. Not until a near fall off a mold-covered log bridging a spongy green swamp did Navitalai volunteer to carry my knapsack. His slow and shy smile said it all—a white woman is next to helpless.

Leaving the bog, we arrived on a grass-covered mound holding a dozen old *bures*, all of them filthy. At no time in this country had I seen such a slum of a village. No sea breeze reached this dank place, and the setting sun did not penetrate the ragged gray smoke rising from rotting thatched roofs. And where were the children? A white woman arriving at an isolated village always brought new crayons and paper and, with luck, chewing gum and candy.

Villages in Fiji have a central commons, the pride of everyone who lives there. This village was covered with scraggly knee-high grass. Where were all the schoolchildren swinging their machetes with lightning speed, caught up in the competition of seeing who cuts the grass the shortest?

Here there were no young women greeting me with their fat, gurgling babies in their arms. No curious toddlers peeked shyly from behind their mothers' *sulus*.

This was the first truly decaying village I had seen in this country. If there was one, there would be more. Rank trashy shrubs grew out of control and invaded the central commons. I shuddered; the lurking night-biting mosquitoes hiding in the tall weeds during the day would have a feast tonight, and I had no mosquito net, only the bottle of insecticide. Walking past a few *bures*, I heard an occasional muted, "Bula bula," from a woman standing in a smoke-grimed doorway. A long time ago this village had withered and possibly without even a struggle.

Why was I here? HQ should have known better than to expect a bank loan to bring cattle or goats here. Everybody understands that a cow needs grass. If a cow was brought here she would break a leg as soon as she left the bush road. Helicopter her in from the road? Goats would go lame with foot rot and would have to be slaughtered before producing young. This place was hell on earth; only the mangroves and insects flourished here. Why were these people here? Were they outcasts or in some sense prisoners? Was this a leper colony? Leprosy was still a danger in this hemisphere.

The sun set and I was trapped for the night. Nothing to do but be polite and somehow muddle through. The chief's wife, spare and delicate, carrying the tiniest of kerosene lamps, met me on her threshhold. She looked more like the chief's mother than his spouse.

Demurely she welcomed me with a, "Iaco mei, Iaco mei." She coughed, trying not to, and I soon knew it was a chronic cough. Almost in a whisper, the woman said, "Sisili," bath, and before I could respond with a, "Thank you; I just need to wash my hands and face," the couple's five-year-old daughter silently took my hand and led me to the stream for my *sisili*.

On this black moonless night, my flashlight showed a rock-strewn stream. During old tribal war days this village site would have been safe from surprise attack, with dense mangroves on two sides and a stream protecting the other sides.

Can anyone bathe while holding a flashlight? I left it inside my knapsack. This meant negotiating the slippery muddy embankment in the dark and bathing in a swirling black stream I chillingly felt but could not see. Cold water quickly enveloped me to my ears, and instantly soap and washcloth, treasured possessions, disappeared before I caught my breath. My child-guide was somewhere in the dark waters with me, but she surely knew where the shallows were. When I climbed up the bank to get dressed I turned on my flashlight and found the child patiently waiting for me beside my knapsack. During my entire visit the child never spoke a word.

Supper in the shadow-filled *bure* of my host family might have been for them a specially fine one but was for the hungry guest a grave disappointment. One dried fish, the size of my hand and about as thick, was shared by six people. Add to this the grainy, tasteless *dalo* washed down by weak warm tea, with no sugar, probably made at dawn.

Before the first meager bite, the chief clasped his hands and mumbled a prayer in a local dialect. I recognized only "Caristio and Ahmen." During supper the teenage daughter of the couple, wearing a white dress, came silently through the darkness and sat next to her mother. The girl did not look at me or speak during supper. I assumed she had walked through the mangroves in the dark from her school somewhere on the road.

"Chief Navitalai, how long have your people lived in this village?"

"It was during the reign of our last great *turanga*."

"Cakambau?"

"*Io, io*. Before he requested the Americans and then the British Queen Victoria colonize our country."

"That was about hundred years ago."

"*Io*. At that time my ancestors had lived in a village near the sea for as long as memory lives."

"During those years your fish for dinner was bigger than this one we eat tonight?"

In the deep shadows of the *bure* Navitalai sat without speaking for a moment. His eyes blinked uneasily at the faint flow of the kerosene lamp. A shy smile parted his lips before he spoke.

"Yes, Miss Barbara, *sa levu ika*, many big fish, eels, turtle eggs, not like here, here *tawa yanga*, bad."

"And many papaws and bananas and coconuts. Your ancestors could have stayed near the sea?"

"*Senga*. Too much fighting. Every month another battle. Every night our young warriors watched in the dark for another attack. Soon the young men were killed, their bodies carried away. They ended up in the *lovo* ovens for ceremonial feasts and *meke*."

Navitalai grimaced with disgust. He raised his hands, palms towards me. He didn't like to talk about his ancestors.

"Can you go back to this village today?"

"*Senga, senga*. It is not the same village now. Only maybe our children can go. But then they must work in the tourist hotel."

"Sounds good to me."

"*Ca senga!* Bad things happen. Our Romulisi, my uncle's son, and our young Lasa, my wife's dead sister's daughter, live there now."

"Where is this village?"

"Your driver who brought you here lives in it. My nephew works at the hotel across the road."

"This is the village of your ancestors?"

"*Io io*. After most of our men were dead the *turanga*, the chief, of our enemy sent a signal by his drum. If my ancestors left at once they would not attack and carry off our young women and children."

Another example of a Fijian unilateral treaty.

The chief continued, "Only a few men were left in our village, too old or too young to fight. That is when my ancestors came here. *Ca, ca*. No one fights to live here. Very bad here."

After dinner the women attempted to entertain me with a *meke*. It was a joyless affair.

In the faint flicker of the kerosene light their hesitant chant-song was about a fly and the eternal but useless struggle to rid their home of this pest. The *bure* was so dim flies might lie drowned in my coconut cup filled with *yanqona*, my gift to them. It was particularly bitter that night, but I forced myself to drink as much as I could. The grainy brown liquid proved to be a useless sleeping potion. The only response was slight numbing of the tongue and lips. After many drinks, to my surprise I found that my hosts understood my rendition of their language very well. It was either the lazy *yanqona* tongue or their *yanqona*-grogged comprehension. Is this why Fijians mumble all the time?

My bed was behind several torn *sulus* draped over roof beams, and it was the Fijian bed reserved for guests. It was also a torture device, a platform of rough wooden planks. No grass mat, nothing, only bare wood to lie on. The floor *imbe* would have been kinder to my bones but was also caked with damp dirt, and picking up *kutu* meant I would give free transport to lice and fleas.

The night was agonizingly long. I spent it fantasizing brightly colored coral reefs with luminescent azure angelfish sliding into caves, eluding me. I slept only minutes at a time before prickly muscle spasms woke me. HQ was stupid to bring me here, and I looked forward to telling them exactly why they were stupid, which is because this village had died long before any of us were born. It had died before our grandparents were born. My hosts ceased to care about their future. They sent their young away as soon as they reached sixteen years of age, when their free education ceased.

The restless night finally over, I carefully folded the *sulu* I had worn when taking my *sisili* in the stream. I left it on the wood bed. It wasn't much, but it was prettier and newer than anything I had seen the night before.

I joined the chief for a morning cup of tea, and he presented me with a high honor, a pair of wild pig tusks, *ilaso*. They were not very long, but his smile was broad as he told me how his semiwild bush dogs had surrounded the boar, confused it, and finally worn it out, so he could take aim and pierce its chest. The boar with the spear imbedded, bleeding from his nose, continued to attack.

Navitalai pointed to a six-foot spear fastened to the rafters. He told the story partly in English, with Fijian when words failed. He had told it many times before and hoped his children would retell it to their children. There weren't many wild pigs left on the island, and they couldn't hide forever. Ancestors of these beasts were the domesticated ones brought to these shores by Captain Cook and others who came to these islands for precious hardwoods.

Navatilai described the frenzy of the beast as it continued to charge, squealing shrilly, tusks slashing but always just missing Navatilai's legs. The dogs kept the wounded beast on the defensive. Finally the chief swung his machete and cut the boar's jugular and the beast went down.

His dogs, sleeping near the entrance, were small-bodied, ribs showing, sores weeping where the flies and fleas feasted. I had seen bush dogs in a pack fighting one another. They moved with lightning speed. These six scrawny dogs knew how to attack the rear of the pig, avoiding the razor-sharp tusks and giving Navitalai opportunity to plunge his spear and swing his machete.

Still kneeling in my host's *bure*, I made my polite *vanaka vaka levu*. The sun was shining, but the inside of the *bure* was musty and dark and the floor *imbe* was torn and soiled. Daylight only detailed more clearly the ravages of poverty. Navitalai's wife was too weary and ill to cut and shred newly gathered grasses to weave new floor *imbe*. In this mangrove eco-system she may also have to walk miles to find the plants.

The *bure* had only one door and no window. When it rained she cooked inside the *bure* regardless of the smoke. In parting, she asked me one question. It was the only sentence the minister's wife spoke during my visit.

"Miss Barbara, please give this Bible to our Lasa. *Vinaka, vinaka*."

The small Bible, limp with mold, its spine cracked, fit into my shirt pocket. There was no need to ask why Lasa had left her birth village. I couldn't wait another minute to get out of there.

* * *

Tables covered with white linens, candles lit in sparkling glass chimneys, teak floors gleaming, a glass of good Scotch in my hand, I was mellowing; life was again good. Sliding wood-paneled screens in the dining room of the hotel were fully opened to a fireball sun dipping into an orange-streaked sea. A caressing breeze, gently tumbling waves, and fronds of palm trees whispering close by—I warmed to the seductive tropical scene. Perhaps HQ could be forgiven. They had no way of knowing the depth of poverty of that remote village.

HQ would be dismayed and without a clue as to how to assist. The only solution was burning the village down and relocating the people. But where would they be welcome? I had to stop thinking about them. I had a few days to indulge in luxury; my bungalow with a soft clean bed, a hot water shower, a balcony looking out toward a reef calling to me. The sea was calm within a natural harbor, and the water swirling around the exposed reef at low tide was only a friendly foam. Tomorrow with flippers I could reach my coral reef within minutes.

My waiter, Romulisi, unsmiling, too thin, stunted in size, stood like a soldier at attention against a wall close to my table. He wore a black tailored *sulu* skirt, white starched shirt and black bow tie. And he was barefoot.

He spoke English, every word carefully pronounced. "Miss Barbara, may I bring you another drink?"

"One more Scotch on ice, thank you."

Earlier in the day, on the drive to the hotel, my Jeep driver had told me that Romulisi lived in the village across the road from the hotel and that he helped plant *tei tei* and gardens of cocoa and helped with the copra crop. The driver called him Romu and said he was chiefly. When Navitalai died, Romu would be the next chief of his birth village, the one I had spent the night in.

Watching Romu, erect and formal, a white napkin draped over his left arm, I had to struggle against another flashback to his bleak birthplace. That cursed village. The harder I tried to escape its ghostly image, the clearer I saw the grimy *bures* and the gray smoke leaking through warped doors and molding thatch roofs. Two young people escaped, Romulisi and also a young girl named Lasa. They both lived in that splendid village across from the hotel where every *bure* looked newly built, the thatch roofs glowed in the sun, and paths spread with white sand were bordered by brightly blossoming ornamental shrubs. The economy of this village depended on this hotel. My driver told me the hotel was owned by a rich and famous Hollywood actor who only came there occasionally and who had several Fijians living with him in his American home.

The Bible—tomorrow I would visit Lasa and give it to her. Tonight was party night. Romu came toward me with a tray holding a new bottle of Inch of Pinch and poured several inches over a tumbler filled with ice cubes.

"The last time I saw Scotch of this quality I was on the other side of the world. Romu, I'm not sure I can afford it."

"*Senga na lenga*, Miss Barbara you spent last night in my old village. Tonight . . . tonight I give you our best Scotch. *Senga na lenga*."

Romu had never anticipated a woman livestock officer. With this Scotch he was giving me a gift, and the Hollywood actor whose private stock I was drinking would never know of it. Of course it must have been Romu who requested a site visit, and soon he would learn that any attempt to breathe life into his decaying village would fail, that not even goats will survive in a mangrove eco-system. How was it possible that Romu had faith and hope for a miracle? Did he know that his aunt very likely had TB? In the morning while drinking my tea in her *bure* she had placed a handkerchief over her mouth when she coughed and when she returned it to her pocket it was spotted with fresh blood.

I sipped my Scotch and watched Romu push his way through swinging doors into the kitchen. Could anyone shape a reality in which Romu actually went back as chief to his decadent home in the swamps? Romu returned with my grilled fish, curried rice, honey-glazed plantain bananas, and steamed tiny curled green ferns, a delicious feast.

Out in the harbor a couple on the deck of their anchored sailing yacht pulled in a dinghy, climbed down a ladder, and leisurely paddled toward the hotel. Their seagoing ship, a gleaming white sixty-footer, flew the flag of New Zealand. The couple pulled their dingy onto the beach and came toward the hotel. The man, middle-aged, and the younger woman were shown by Romu to a table next to mine.

The man spoke with a strong New Zealand accent. "Good evening, Romu. Bring us our usual cocktail. What do you suggest for our entrée?"

His blond sunbleached hair, his tanned and leathery skin prematurely wrinkled, he filled the dining room with his loud, coarse voice. The woman, a long-haired brunette, willowy and more than a decade younger than the man, wore no makeup. She looked like a supermodel from back home. If she was the sailor's first mate, it was perhaps not at the helm of his oceangoing mansion. During the evening the lady spoke only rarely and then always with a flashing smile and in the manner of a conspirator.

Romu brought two cocktails and the man asked, "Have you seen my nephew lately? I was hoping he would join us for dinner tonight?"

"*Io*, Mr. Campbell. He left a message for you at the desk. He will join you soon, and he will be bringing a guest."

"Thank you, Romu. He didn't by any chance tell you if our guest is male or female?"

"No, Mr. Campbell, he did not."

By nightfall there were only a few tables vacant. Guests sauntered in from their bungalows for their evening drinks and dinner and the waiters greeted them by name.

Romu led a young Fijian girl and her escort, a man with hair the color of corn silk, to Mr. Campbell's table but did not move the chair out for the girl. Romu stood by

Campbell's side while he ordered another round of cocktails and then quickly left. The girl's entrance into the dining room did not go unnoticed. Judging by her graceful walk, head held high, and her amber eyes not looking to the left or right, she was comfortable with all the attention she attracted. Her closely cropped hair fringed a face of exquisite doll-like features. Her neck delicately arched, her shoulders bare, her cobalt blue dress hugged the body of a dancer. With her skin a shimmering mocha, only her hair, crisp black curls, identified her as Fijian.

"Good to see both of you again," Campbell said, "Michael, has it really been a year?"

"At least. The sailing was smooth all the way from Christ Church, was it?"

Campbell put his arm around the brunette and said, "Just about perfect. Ne'er a squall, fair winds, star-filled nights, navigating instruments behaved, and the best mate a man could wish for. Now tell me, Michael, what's been happening in your life? Your parents haven't heard from you in a while."

Michael sat at his table facing mine, and his answer was greeted by Campbell with an outburst. The Fijian girl's back was to me, so if she spoke I was not able to hear her words.

"A baby! Michael, my boy, this is a surprise!" shouted Campbell. "Your parents didn't tell us. Well now, that does put new color on things, doesn't it."

"Not much. Not really. The baby is living in the village and—"

Romu came with a tray of drinks and took their dinner order. Michael looked relieved at the interruption.

The barman played taped music from the 1940s and 1950s, beginning with *South Pacific*, then on to Glenn Miller's, Tommy Dorsey's and Woody Herman's slow dance music. Michael and his girl left the table for the dance floor. Her face, close to his, held an amused and confident smile. Michael's open hand on her back, below her waist, held her close. They danced as only lovers do in a world of their own design. She was the only nonwhite guest, and the eyes of other diners lingered on her every bit as long as mine did. Molu, waiting by the bar for an order to be filled, watched the couple with a sad and resigned expression.

Molu came to fill my water glass, and I asked him who the lovely young girl was.

"Lasa, her name is Lasa. We are cousins."

He turned quickly away and filled the glasses at Campbell's table.

So this dazzling young creature, to whom I would present the Bible, was born and raised in that dingy spectral village. Her aunt was worried about her, and with good reason. When Lasa returned to her table I saw no wedding ring on her fingers. The baby Campbell was surprised to hear about—her baby?

"Miss Barbara, would you like an after-dinner sherry?" Romu's voice was insistent.

"Thank you, yes, Romulisi. Wait, please. So Lasa is your cousin. I have something her aunt wanted me to give to her—I don't have it with me. When do you think would be a good time for me to visit her tomorrow?"

Mulu's eyes concentrated on the floor before he answered.

"She is home in the afternoon . . . before . . ." He hesitated again. "She bathes the baby and puts him down for a nap in the afternoon. Excuse me."

Glossy color photos of Lasa's new village, Koro-ni-Wa, Village by the Sea, are often found in travel agents' brochures, luring the tired rich out of dreary northern cities in winter: "Here, time has stood still, untouched by the chaos of the modern world. The pace is languid, the people always smiling and cheerful. Village life is a carefree one."

In Koro-ni-Wa everything is in proper order. Tourists paying thousands of dollars to stay at the hotel across the road are tempted to wander into this tropical paradise but are warned at check-in not to enter the village unless invited for a *meke*.

The central commons is mowed with a petrol-fueled mower, every *bure* newly thatched; community showers and bathrooms are whitewashed concrete. Diesel generators churn out kilowatt hours until exactly 11:30 P.M. every night. Instead of the traditional meeting house for the ancient traditional ceremonies, a new white Methodist church with hardwood pews was built for meetings called by the chief, Christian rights of passage, and Sunday services.

Lasa's *vale* was the first one just off the main road, and when I knocked on the open front door and called out her name a masculine voice answered.

"Miss Barbara, *laco mai, laco mai*." Romulisi motioned me inside. "Lasa took her baby to meet Michael's uncle. She won't be back until late."

The bure was a brightly lit three-room bungalow with all the basic modern kitchen appliances. A chromium high chair, playpen, and a new crib were the only baby furniture I had ever seen in a Fijian village. On the kitchen table lay an old copy of *Cosmopolitan* Magazine and empty Gerber baby food jars.

"It's this Bible, Romu; Lasa's aunt wanted her to have it—it could use a bit of repairing, don't you think? Perhaps you have some glue and paper?"

We were both embarrassed at the condition of this Bible.

Romu placed it on top of the *Cosmopolitan* Magazine and said, "*Io, io,* the hotel has some. I will fix."

"This is a comfortable and pretty home for Lasa and her baby. How old is the baby?"

"Only six months."

The silences were lengthening after each interchange.

"Lasa's aunt, she knows . . . about the . . . the baby?"

"The jungle grapevine—she knows."

The word *meddling* bounced around in my head. Did I have the right to tell Molu about his aunt being ill? The right to inform him that his birth village was hell on earth? Even if he was going to be the next chief of his village, did he have any right to make decisions today?

Without being invited to sit down at the kitchen table I pulled out a chair and sat.

I motioned Molu to the other chair and said, "Please Romu. Your aunt is very sick."

"I know."

"Her little girl and the older daughter, they need to be moved away from the village—as soon as possible."

"It may be too late."

"That may be—and then again, perhaps there is a chance."

Molu stared down at the roses on the plastic tablecloth.

"Is there an extended family in this village, a family without children who might take them in?"

More silence.

"*Io, io,* we have an elderly couple living here."

"Could you talk to them?"

"If I ask them, they must do what I say. They cannot say no to me. They are family."

His thin shoulders slumped forward. We sat without talking. I got up and looked out the door at the palms on the beach gently swaying, the surf lazy. A maid came out of the hotel laundry pushing a red wheelbarrow piled high with white sheets and bath towels. She stopped at a hibiscus shrub, picked a white blossom, and pushed it into her hair. Bringing children here would save them but in all likelihood hasten the death of their mother.

Romu's voice was only a whisper: "It can be done."

"Romu, do you really believe we can bring livestock to your old village?"

He never answered.

"You left several years before Lasa did?"

"*Io*."

"Lasa looks healthy and she looks happy. Is it not right to move the children out?"

"Every payday I send money to my village for food."

Romu, a one-man welfare agency, he can save his village?

"Michael will never marry Lasa." Romu continued, "He has a wife and children in New Zealand."

"He will abandon Lasa?"

"He must stay here—he manages his family's copra, banana, and cocoa plantations. His New Zealand wife came and left."

"His family owns land, *Matangali* land?"

"His great-grandfather bought the land with worthless gifts to a chief he made drunk. Michael's land brings in the best cocoa on Vanua Levu. His family stole this land."

"So Lasa will always be wife number two?"

"*Io, io, san dina*. Still . . . she lives . . . She lives . . . . She has a fat baby."

Molu left the table, carefully set his chair against the wall, and walked out the door.

As he passed me, for the first time he looked me in the eyes, and he said, "When Michael is old and he dies there will be another and another—"

167

"And your old village, Molu, will you return?"

Perhaps he never heard the question. He crossed the road and walked through the back door into the hotel.

15
Dr. Tomba

Ili knocked softly on my door, put down both pails of water on the floor mat, turned slowly, and walked back down the path toward her *bure*. No cheerful "bula bula," no gossip from school, no sidelong glance at the candy jar, nothing. Ili ambled down the path, her tall, slender body slumping and her arms dangling wearily at her sides.

"Ili, wait. Are you all right? Wait!"

Ili turned around to face me, and I found the whites of the child's eyes were as yellow as mustard.

"Ili, you are sick. Has your mother seen you this afternoon?"

"*Segna, segna*, I only now come home from school."

"You're very late coming home. How do you feel?"

"*Wakewake*, Miss Barbara, very tired."

"You should have seen the school nurse while you were there. Now you will have a very long walk back to school tomorrow to see her."

"Miss Barbara, I did see her. She says to go to clinic and be put in their hospital."

"What did she say was wrong with you?"

"Bad blood, she say."

"You must do what she said. Did she say something that sounded like *hepatitis*?"

"Something like that. I don't want to go. I've never been away from my family."

Ili's eyes filled with tears. Her forehead felt clammy to the touch. I followed Ili to her *bure*. Maria and Tomaci and their six children were sitting around their dinner, cloth spread on the *imbe*, eating supper.

As soon as Maria looked at her daughter, her face grew serious and she muttered, "*Dra ca ca.*"

"Yes, Maria, it does look like bad blood disease. Poor Ili feels really sick."

Maria asked Ili why she didn't go to the school nurse. Ili sat down next to her mother and cried while her mother scolded. A plan was finally worked out with Ili tearfully agreeing. In the morning I planned to meet with Suni at the local agricultural station. On the way I could take Ili to the clinic for treatment. We would walk to the road and wait for a bus to take us into the nearby small town with a clinic.

"Maria, why is Ili so frightened? She will be close by. It's not as if she is going far away to the city."

"Ili thinks people go to *Vale ni mata* to die, Miss Barbara, only to die. They never come home again."

I tried to explain to Ili. "The hospital is called house of death and sickness because a long long time ago, before there were new drugs to cure people of disease, people often did die. But today only the very old, the very sick, cannot be cured with many new drugs. You are young and healthy, and soon you will be home again. Today the name given the hospital doesn't mean anything."

Ili leaned against Maria and tried to be brave.

I continued. "Sometimes even names or titles given to people mean nothing at all. Just like I am called livestock officer. Do you think that I am an army officer in charge of cattle and goats and pigs with guns around their waists and that I teach them how to shoot and go to war?"

Ili stopped crying long enough to giggle through her tears but then started crying again.

"Ili, the clinic will give you medicine. You are going to be well enough to go back to school in a few weeks. You are not so very sick. You will see. The nurses will spoil you and give you lots of attention. You will have your meals brought to you in bed. You will see."

Ili cried uncontrollably.

Ili lay propped up in a clean bed in a small ward with other patients, some also with the yellow cast to their eyes. Dr. Tomba, a tall, heavy black man, came toward us walking like a large, soft, lumbering animal. On his feet he wore rubber thong sandals that with each step flopped noisily against the rough wood floors. His barrel chest permitted tying only the top strings of his white gown behind his thick neck, and his white scrub trousers reached midcalf on his bare legs.

His large, round, somber eyes peered down at his wary patient. He placed Ili's small hand in his and silently waited for her to stop weeping.

"Ili, you have come just in time for a nice lunch to be served to you in bed. Have you ever had breakfast, lunch, and dinner served to you in bed before? No? You will like it so much you won't want to go home to your *bure* again."

This giant of a man examined Ili gently, not touching her bare skin, only palpating her abdomen through her hospital gown. Soon Ili calmed, her eyes scanning his broad, placid face. I had never seen Ili look directly into the eyes of her father, her brothers, or her uncles. But now she was clearly fascinated with this large gentle man. She was not afraid of him.

Dr. Tomba motioned me to follow him, and we left Ili in the hands of a young, smiling Fijian nurse.

"Barbara, the child will not be here too long. Her type of hepatitis we can treat and release her maybe in a week. I have to do some blood tests before I can be sure."

"I'll tell that to her parents. They will be relieved. And now I must let you get back to your work, Dr. Tomba. Thank you very much."

"Barbara, wait. Come to my office. We have something to discuss. Come."

I followed him through a larger ward of ten beds and heard my name called by one of the women patients.

A young woman waved and said, "Miss Barbara! *Bula, bula*. Have you come to see me, too?"

I couldn't remember ever seeing the girl before, but her abdominal bulge under the sheet could only mean she was close to delivering a baby.

"You must be the wife of one of our scheme farmers. I'm sorry I don't remember your name."

"No, it is my father who is a farmer on the cattle scheme. I am Arlene. You spoke to us in our village about . . . about . . ."

Arlene's eyes drifted over to Dr. Tomba standing in the doorway. He was watching and listening to us. Arlene's eyes blurred with tears, and I then remembered the first and only time I had met Arlene. She was one of Principal Lania's schoolgirls in the pretty village a half-day's walk from my *bure*. The village that had never had an unmarried young girl pregnant before or a woman pregnant whose husband had been away for two years.

"Arlene, when I'm finished talking to Dr. Tomba I'll come back and visit with you. We will have a nice chat. That is, unless you're going to be otherwise occupied."

My attempt at humor was wasted on Arlene. Tears shimmered in her eyes.

Dr. Tomba's office was not much larger than a concrete walk-in closet with a window. The fan on the windowsill swung in its arc, setting mounds of files and loose papers trembling on top of a battered remnant of a metal World War II government issue desk. There was only one chair. The seat appeared too small, the frame too weak to support the heavy bulk of Dr. Tomba. He was six and a half feet tall, and when I sat down he towered over me.

He gathered up a load of medical reports, hugged them to his chest, went out to the nurse's station, and dropped them noisily on her desk. He returned, closed the door, sat down on his desk, and turned toward me. His face wore a rueful expression.

His deep voice resonated in the small room. He spoke to me as a superior would speak to a schoolchild in his care.

"Barbara, you spent several days at Principal Lania's village talking to the girls about planned parenthood, as you describe it in the States. You know about the pregnant teenager you were talking to just now."

"She was one of the girls, yes."

His eyes were not symmetrical. One was centered and aligned to look into mine, but his other eye focused at some point beyond me. While he spoke, one eye never left my face. But the errant eye slowly moved sideways and upward within its lid and partially disappeared. At this point Dr. Tomba blinked owl-like, and when he opened his eyes the eye was again focused centrally. But not for long. Involuntarily I found myself watching the traveling eye. I was fascinated by the display. How did he do it? With a life of its own the eye disappeared into its lid until he blinked and brought it back.

"I understand that Suni is your superior here in our little town."

"Yes, he is. However, during the past several months I have worked more closely with Suva HQ."

"You have had lunch with Suni in his home."

"Only rarely. Sometimes his mother cooks lunch for me when I come into town. There's no decent restaurant."

"You have driven to Suva with Suni."

"Yes, of course. We attend meetings at HQ."

His accented English was not that of a Fijian. His *a*'s were long and drawn out, with some of his words clipped short.

"You and he spent a weekend at his village."

"His mother and sisters and brothers were with us the entire time. He installed one of the first hydro-electric plants on the Rewa River. He wanted to show me—he hoped I could find venture capital for more plants."

The doctor sighed heavily and said, "Suni's mother is a tough old Fijian woman. She is the widow of the chief of Suni's village. She takes very good care of her son, a chiefly son."

I tired of the effort of concentrating on his one good eye while the other played hide and seek. More important, Dr. Tomba was breaking with all village culture. He was looking directly into my eyes, the eyes of a white woman. He both irritated and fascinated me. I also resented his talking to me as a headmaster would to a subservient child. Did he enjoy placing me on the defensive? Finally I concentrated on his immense black feet. His list of facts was puzzling. What was he trying to tell me?

"Before you came, Barbara, I treated an elderly Indian woman involved in a pedestrian accident. She was hit by a government vehicle. She eventually died of pneumonia, not a rare death in the tropics. When she was brought to us by her family it was because she had suffered several broken ribs in the accident."

"Dr. Tomba, I don't know what any of this has to do with me."

His basso voice continued as if I hadn't spoken. "The driver was going too fast, he hit her, and then he did not stop to help her. It was early evening and the Indian woman recognized the driver."

"So?"

"She said it was Suni."

"He does not appear to me to be the sort of man who would hit someone with a car and not stop to give aid."

"Not even if it was an Indian he hit? And not even if he had been drinking in the local bar?"

"Was there a police investigation?"

"The local police chief filed his report."

"And Suni was found not to have been in the vicinity?"

"No. Suni was found to be the passenger, and Beni was found to be the driver to the government vehicle that hit the woman. Beni had also been drinking in the bar."

Dr. Tomba slowly slid his body off the desk and turned toward the door. "Beni said he was the driver. He had his license revoked for one year, and the death of the Indian woman, my patient, was officially listed as death by pneumonia. Case closed."

He opened the door to leave, hesitated, turned around, and again faced me. In the tiny office he was forced to stand too close to me. It was a stretch for me to look into his face. From his height, his gaze lingered on me. For a brief moment I expected he might touch me, but he never did.

"Barbara, the lymph nodes in your neck are swollen. Do something about your illness and do it soon."

He quietly closed the door behind him.

I sat in Dr. Tomba's office several minutes thinking about what he had originally referred to as having a "discussion" with me. He had made several facts evident to me: His opinion of Beni and Suni was negative. Obviously, the doctor thought the old Indian woman would not have gotten pneumonia and died if she hadn't been injured in the accident. He said I had lumps on my neck. So what? They had been there for more months than I cared to remember. All it meant was that my immune system was kicking in. That was a good sign. So what?

For Dr. Tomba to know so much about my movements was a bit of a surprise. But it shouldn't have been. I was the oddity in this closed culture, and every bit of new gossip was a wonderful treat to be shared around the *yanqona* bowl.

The only truly disturbing news was the fact that Suni and Beni were drinking buddies and that Beni had taken the rap for the accident caused by his boss. This explained Suni's ambivalence and inability to govern Beni and control him. The police chief, who had asked to share my nonexistent hoard of marijuana, was a very close friend of Suni; the only other ranking government official in the small town. It was easy for him to change the name of the driver of the government vehicle.

Arlene was sitting up in bed with her hands spread over her large abdomen. Was she happy about her coming baby? Was she worried about not being married? I decided it was best to keep the conversation nonspecific. Just one more case of parthenogenesis in the Christian world, i.e., the ability to produce individuals from unfertilized eggs, explained to us as wee children as immaculate conception. Arlene was in no shape for a friendly chat. Her contractions were coming close together, and she asked me to send the nurse to her.

At the nurse's station I found her rifling through the disorderly mound of Dr. Tomba's files. She had tucked a few files under one arm and made three stacks on her desk, and the rest she piled on a chair. I told her Arlene needed her, and she said the doctor was aware of the girl's contractions and would take care of her.

"You need a filing clerk."

"Miss Barbara, we don't even have enough filing cabinets. File clerks? We, the nurses, are the file clerks. In this clinic, cardboard boxes become file cabinets."

She lowered her voice. "And our doctor is no help at all. He lets them pile up on his desk until . . . this." The nurse shrugged her shoulders and groaned.

I risked a personal question: "Dr. Tomba's accent . . . I can't place him. Is he from New Zealand or Australia?"

"Senga, senga. He is from Cambridge, Miss Barbara."

"Ah, yes, of course he is from England."

"*Senga, senga*. He is from your country. He has a degree from a university in your country."

"Cambridge, Massachusetts?"

"*Io, io*. Miss Barbara, would you bring me Dr. Tomba's desk chair? I need to make one more stack."

"You really do need a file cabinet."

"Dr. Tomba won't order file cabinets. He has a memory like an elephant. He only has to read a medical file once, write his diagnosis, give orders for medication, and he will forever remember. We do not have memories like him, but he will not listen to us. We are not geniuses like him."

"I have noticed that he talks but does not listen."

"*Io, io*. He does not have to listen. He sees. He sees everything. I think it is with the eye that wants to hide all the time. He sees things no one else sees. He knows everything that there is to know. But he never asks questions. He is a genius who will drive us all crazy, and very soon."

"He will probably not stay in Fiji very long. Perhaps he is here as a missionary?"

"*Segna*, Miss Barbara, he is not like yourself. You will go home, but not him. A very, very long time back he took out citizenship in Fiji. He has built a little *bure* behind the clinic."

"He will not return to his home in the States?"

"Who knows? But he is . . ." She hesitated, looked for the right English word and not finding it. "He is *maqosa*, he is a very good doctor. This clinic has never had such a good doctor before. Even the Brits were not as good at delivering babies. And he saves the sick. Only one death all year. He is a genius. But sometimes we think he is a crazy genius."

"He doesn't sound even a little crazy to me. Perhaps mildly eccentric."

"*Io, io*. He does go a little crazy. Sometimes he is a wild elephant. An old Indian woman who was hit by a government Jeep died last year, and he went into his office and broke his chair into a thousand pieces. He went crazy."

"He does look a little like a big, lumbering elephant at that."

"*Io, sa levu*. And when he sees a patient for the first time he knows whether he can save the life. When he sees he can save the life he will stay up all night and nurse the patient himself."

"He should be my doctor instead of my going into Suva and wasting several days."

"*Io*, Miss Barbara. But please do not come to us if you think you will die. We do not have enough chairs as it is. He is a very good doctor, but he will not buy file cabinets. He orders steam ovens to sterilize needles and syringes, but he will not buy file cabinets."

"And let us hope you will not have to buy many new chairs for a very long time."

"Miss Barbara, are all American doctors this crazy?"
"Perhaps only the great ones come to countries like yours."

16
Fortitude or Folly?

I left the clinic, but without a bus stop in sight I started walking, in the hope some driver would offer me a lift. There was little traffic, so I walked with my back to oncoming cars. The road was narrow and whenever I heard traffic behind me I stepped into the brushy safety zone.

My so-called discussion with Dr. Tomba was troubling. Suni was indeed a wild card. For the past year I had preferred to think of him as a lazy, harmless bureaucrat. Now he was a lazy alcoholic bureaucrat who, in Dr. Tomba's perception, had killed an Indian woman. Months ago when Suni drove the Jeep back from Suva HQ he had finished off close to three quarts of beer and I thought nothing of it. I drank the other quart. With the dust, the heat, and the long wasteful day at HQ, I was grateful for the Jeep cocktail hour. Driving with Suni would now come to an abrupt halt. The open-air buses filled my lungs and eyes and every pore in my face with sand and diesel smoke. There was only one solution, and that would be to stop attending regional meetings at HQ. Nothing ever came of those dreary sessions anyhow.

I was engrossed in my thoughts, and not until I heard the roaring engine of a truck close behind did I jump off the road to safety. I faced the truck as it was headed toward the spot I had been. I saw the driver's head turn abruptly to look across the road to a small house that appeared to be vacant. But at the instant the driver's head turned toward the house, a woman backed out carrying a large load of laundry. The driver of the truck immediately swerved back toward the center of the road, accelerated, skidding in the dust, and disappeared around a curve. When the truck careened past me I saw the logo painted on the cab door: FIJIAN MINISTRY OF AGRICULTURE. The driver was a small Fijian man wearing a red visored cap and large sunglasses.

I slid my knapsack off my shoulders, set it in the grass, and sat on it. My hands were shaking and I felt sick. I watched the Fijian housewife across the road take sheets out of her basket and delicately impale them on the jagged ends of fence posts and barbed wire. Why didn't the woman's husband stretch a rope between two trees? In a breeze the clothes would tear on the fence and the dust of the road would settle on the laundry.

At first the woman was unaware of my watching her. When she glanced across the road and found my eyes intent on her, she smiled broadly and called, "*Bula, bula*, Miss Barbara!" and continued her work.

Did the driver of the truck fall asleep at the wheel and the truck was out of control? But then why did the driver turn his head sharply toward the house as the woman backed out with her laundry basket? Why did he not stop and apologize for frightening me? Why did he not stop and give me a lift? Within many miles there was only one white woman with red hair carrying a knapsack walking towards the agricultural station. He must have known who I was.

The housewife carefully draped a girl's blue school uniform just like Ili's over her dilapidated fence. If she hung it up just right, maybe she would not have to iron the dress. The woman was unaware that a life only a few feet from her had been spared by the simple act of her coming out of her house to hang up her laundry. The woman picked up her empty handwoven basket made of palm leaves and waved.

"Miss Barbara! *Laco mai, laco mai. Endua na billo* tea?"

Yes, I very much needed a cup of tea. I would give a full day's pay for a nice cup of tea. But the woman was only rendering the traditional polite invitation. She didn't really intend or want me to accept. This woman, who had saved my life, now offered me a cup of tea. Let her go. This woman didn't have time to waste chatting over a cup of tea. I didn't have time. I had almost lost all time. I crossed the road and thanked the woman for her invitation. Then I slung my knapsack over my shoulder, and it felt heavier than it did before. I continued walking. Now I walked facing oncoming traffic and a weariness slowed my steps. Dr. Tomba was probably right, the lumps on my neck needed to be looked at. Dr. Tomba, was his nurse right? He saw everything. Could he see what no one else could see? Could the crazy doctor from Cambridge, Massachusetts, with one restless eye, a man with the memory of an elephant who smashed chairs when a patient died, see before there was anything to see? When he watched me and Arlene chatting at her bedside did he see what was to happen to me today? And also tomorrow?

One more irrelevant meeting with Suni was a waste. There was a small and modest hotel in town with three or four rooms and food only acceptable to someone living on a starvation diet. The Indian family who owned and managed the place made their profits on Saturday nights when the Fijians came out of the bush and drank themselves silly with Fiji Bitters. This was the bar where Suni and Beni had done likewise.

I checked myself in, had a meal of cold curried rice and chewy goat meat served by an Indian woman, and then went directly to bed. The fact that it was only one o'clock in the afternoon was irrelevant. Another fact was the irrelevance of my job description as livestock officer. The futility of bringing my standards of cattle management into a country determined to shed itself of all that was both right and wrong during its century of British colonial rule.

I was awakened several hours later by an insistent knock on my door. The Indian woman who had served me lunch asked me to quickly get dressed and follow her. Standing outside on the lawn, Mr. Singh, the owner of the hotel, was talking to a young man. The man was excited, waving his arms around helplessly, and I understood not one word of his Hindi.

"Miss Barbara," said Mr. Singh, "please listen to this young sugarcane farmer. He says his Brahman cow is lying on the ground and can't get up."

"I have only one cow," the farmer said, "and until an hour ago she was healthy and her three-day-old calf was nursing her, and then all of a sudden she was staggering and then she collapsed."

"You need a vet. You don't me; you need to get her medicine. You don't have much time. If it is what I think it is, you only have a few hours and then it will be too late."

"We telephoned here from the hotel, and the vet says he cannot come until tomorrow morning. He can't."

"Tell me if this was the cow's first or second calf?"

"Her second calf. She never had a problem delivering. The birth was an easy one."

"Is she in good condition? Does she have good grass? Has she been healthy? Have you taken her temperature?"

"Yes, yes, she is fat; she is healthy. No, I don't have a thermometer."

In all likelihood the cow was suffering what old-timers called milk fever, which was one more misnomer. The temperature of the new mother plummets as the disease hits with lightning speed, often not giving the farmer time to save the animal's life. My thermometer had its own padded pocket in my backpack, but I never carried any medicines. The least I could do was follow the worried young man to his farm and have a look.

This Brahman cow was one of the most beautiful specimens I had seen in Fiji. She was white, with a gentle shading of gray on her face. She might have weighed well over a thousand pounds. She was large-boned and whoever was responsible for tracking her pedigree had done a near-perfect job. Her calf was also a beauty and was being restrained with a rope around its neck by the farmer's young daughter. Surrounding the sick animal was the entire family, at least three generations, all the women in colorful clean saris and the men in white baggy trousers gathered at the ankle. The cow was lying on her brisket with her head on the ground in a tortured position. Her muzzle was a crusty dry black and her eyes were dull, but if she was not unconscious there was a small chance of saving her. I took her temperature and found that it was more than four degrees too low. She did have symptoms of hypocalcemia.

The textbooks warn against drenching a cow in this stage of the disease. The fluid could end up in her lungs as she could not swallow. The textbooks only advise introducing up to five hundred cubic centimeters of five minerals into the body with a large-gauge hypodermic needle. The closest one was more than an hour away at Dr. Tomba's clinic, and his having all the necessary medicines would be most unlikely. What would I do if this was my cow and I knew she only had a few hours to live? I would try to save her. I was reduced to the use of a six-foot length garden hose lubricated with Vaseline, introduced into the cow's esophagus and gently slid down her gullet toward her stomach.

I asked the women to bring me one cup of honey or molasses, several tablespoons of table salt, all the milk they had in the house, either powdered or whole, all the milk of magnesia they could get their hands on, and water. The last mineral needed was potassium. My mind went blank, Potassium, what would an Indian family have that was loaded with potassium? Of course, the banana. How does one get half a dozen bananas down a garden hose into the stomach of a cow that looked like she was comatose?

At least half a dozen women with their colorful saris billowing around them disappeared into various houses, talking to one another as they ran. They looked like a party of pretty butterflies. What was all that nonsense Suni spouted about Indians having no feelings for cattle? That Indians only cared about their ugly little goats? This Indian family was doing whatever it took to save their cow.

Within a few minutes all the necessary ingredients lay before me on a tray, including a watering can. With a rounded club a few bananas were reduced to mush and added to two gallons of milk and water, honey, salt, and a whole bottle of milk of magnesia. I swirled and mixed this brew with my hand and found I could add a few more mashed-up bananas.

Two men raised the cow's head as four men raised her forequarters off the ground. With the garden hose fitted around the neck of the watering can, I raised it and poured its contents as slowly as possible into the cow. Was the hose in her esophagus or her trachea? I prayed the contents were on its way into her stomach and not her lungs. With my free hand I stroked her throat as hard as I could and felt a rhythmic trembling vibration. I breathed my first sigh of relief. The cow's reflexes were slow but intact. She was actually swallowing. By this time the effort of holding several gallons of liquid head-high had reduced my arms to quivering, but I was afraid to let anyone else pour the contents. It seemed to take forever. Too fast and we could drown her.

With rolled-up gunnysacks placed on either side of the cow we were able to support her on her brisket. If she lay down on her side she would get pneumonia. All the blankets in the houses were draped over her body. The men were told that the cow needed to be watched all night. They needed to sleep in shifts. She must be kept warm, and she must not lie on her side.

Returning to the hotel, Mr. Singh took one look at me and told me to follow him to the bar, where he handed me a double shot of Scotch. Certainly this Indian wasn't as penurious as the Fijians make them all out to be. But both races did share the same talent for instant news gathering. Within a few hours the Indian community knew there was a livestock officer in the little hotel.

I slept fitfully all night. I had done exactly what the textbooks said not to do. Was there any other way to get those five ingredients into the cow? I must try to always carry a large hypodermic needle and the necessary ingredients in my knapsack. This was a common disease and the easiest to cure with simple but timely treatment. If the cow died, my reputation was permanently damaged and within hours HQ in Suva would know it. If I had done nothing, the cow would certainly have been dead by nightfall. This was a no-win situation at a time in my life when there did not seem to be any win-wins.

I had nightmare after nightmare all night. I saw the beautiful cow a skeleton lying in the dust. I saw her body covered with diesel fuel and three generations of Indians all holding matches to her, as Indians never bury, only cremate. Near Suva there are days the air is clouded with white smoke from the Indian crematorium, and the acrid smell lingers well into the night.

I woke with the words, "Miss Barbara, wake up! Please wake up!" shouted through the window of my room. Only the head of the Indian could be seen outlined by a dawning day behind him.

"What is it, for heaven's sake? What do you want?"

"You must come now, right away. It is the cow. You must come."

The Indian farmer and I ran into his compound, and I fully expected to find one cow in her last moments of life. What I saw was the entire clan standing in a row behind a huge pile of blankets and smiling.

"Miss Barbara, the cow is gone; see, the cow is gone."

"Where is she? She can't just be gone!"

"Look over there in the sugercane field. See her? She is eating sugarcane, and her calf is nursing her. Do you see her? She is healthy again. Early this morning she got up, mooed for her calf, and straightaway went to the sugarcane field."

He was ever so right. One beautiful, elegant pearly white Brahman cow was chewing her way through a small new-growth sugarcane farm. If I hadn't been so intimidated by these handsomely draped Indian women, I would have run to the cow and given her a big hug. Just as well. The Brahman cow with a new calf is protective and probably would have tried to kill me.

* * *

Suni sat across from me at the hotel while I ate breakfast. What I had to say to him had to be said out of earshot of his Indian and Fijian office staff.

"Suni, unless you can assign me a coworker I'm leaving the scheme."

He showed no surprise. All he said was, "When?"

"Tomorrow I'll be in Suva for a medical checkup. If my stay is longer than a few days I'll have Richard call you. By that time he will also know I need a coworker."

Suni lit a cigarette and looked out the window. If he was disappointed, he didn't show it. I half-expected him to remind me that my job never included drenching a cow that did not live on my scheme. I was fully ready to remind him that he would let any animal die rather than help save one belonging to an Indian.

"HQ should send you a coworker. As for assigning one from my office, that is out of the question."

"You have no one assigned to you in your office who can work with me? No one at all?"

"That is correct, no one."

Always unasked questions hung between Suni and myself. Suni had lost all control over Beni; however, I knew there were other staff members working out of his office who could take on added work. Was he showing every sign that he was impotent to make administrative decisions? Or was he relieved at seeing the last of this American *bulama-cow* lady?

"As you wish, Suni, as you wish."

* * *

The dangerously close encounter with a government vehicle on the road the day before was the final straw for me. I needed to survive; martyrdom was never an option. I left the hotel, returned to my *bure*, packed my knapsack with as many clothes I could, the way sailors do, rolled tight as sausages, and walked out of the bush. My nighttime fevers drained me, my sore throat worsened, and chronic weariness kept me away from farm rounds.

* * *

The doctor in Suva examined me and sent me to the local hospital for a complete blood work-up. The specimens would be sent to Australia for culturing, etc. No, he had no definitive diagnosis except that I was sick and one month late getting a preventive hepatitis shot. He ordered complete bedrest for six weeks to two months; losing twenty-five pounds in a short period of time was grounds enough to go to bed.

At the hospital the Indian doctor asked no questions, just drew two vials of blood, and then his phone rang. He placed the vials on the windowsill with the noonday sun full on my congealing blood. He answered the phone, speaking Hindi, laughed, and promptly forgot I was in his office. I rose from the chair, and he impatiently waved me toward the door. I fought a strong impulse to rescue my blood specimen to place it in the refrigerator next to his desk. I would never have treated a blood specimen from one of my cows with such a cavalier attitude. How much did a round-trip ticket to Sydney cost, to walk into a hospital and give a blood specimen not cooked in the sun? Perhaps Ili was more right than wrong when she referred to a Fijian hospital as a house of death.

I moved into a one-room apartment with a tiny kitchen in a hotel overlooking the Port of Suva. Sitting up in bed, I watched freighters and cruise ships dock and noisily unload containers, and cargo from all over the world. This free entertainment should have been pleasant, but it meant nothing to me. I missed working my job, the soothing murmurs of the jungle, the mumbling of twenty-one farmers, all those needy cows, and the quiet order of village life. I missed going *tropo*.

Friends brought more than fifty books, which I read and promptly forgot their focus. For a time the weariness accelerated. Walking down one flight of stairs to make a phone call was as hard for me as it would have been to walk a mile through shoulder-high water. When I tried to swallow food, the ulcerated throat constricted and I choked.

The nurse shrugged her shoulders when visiting every two weeks. She said the white blood count was still abnormally high and no one knew why. They might send another blood sample to Australia for analysis and wait and see for another week or so. If I got worse, I would have to be medi-vacked to Hawaii; the local hospital was out of the question. Also, Hawaii was closer to the States.

For weeks I lay in bed, weightless and floating. It might have been due to the pain medications or the undiagnosed illness. The thought of Brucellosis and TB floated in and out of my mind. Helping deliver a calf, I had been sprayed in the face with all sorts of contaminants.

Six weeks in bed and the fever finally became only intermittent and I did my own food shopping. The weariness was still a factor, and I was forced to make the decision that returning to the bush, even with a coworker, was out of the question.

Richard came to my apartment and agreed to install me in his office, with a desk, with duties that would keep me busy for at least the next six months, as his paperwork on top of all the TB and Brucellosis testing was too much for him. Apparently TB testing on my scheme had revealed a little over 25 percent of 500 cattle were ill. This bit of news did nothing for my spirits. My worst fears had been proven correct. The abbatoir was working overtime, the farmers were mad at the *bulamacow* lady, and the only good bit of news was that Beni was no longer assigned as a livestock officer. Where was he living? Probably in town with his *taxi*. Richard didn't want the conversation about Beni to proceed. As I had another question on my lips, Richard quickly excused himself. He said his wife and two daughters were waiting for him in the car and that it was parked in the sun.

Two months after I left my *bure* I returned to gather up personal belongings and with the help of a few farmers loaded them on a bus headed into Suva. My neighbors were too polite to ask why I was leaving. Maria and Ili wept silently. I never saw my Fijian family again.

17
A Desk Job

The government-owned apartment became my home until I left Fiji. For the first time I enjoyed running water and a shower with only cold water and a *vale lailai* with twentieth-century plumbing. The concrete-block apartment had two rooms, whitewashed, each with a bare lightbulb hanging from the ceiling. There was a doll-sized refrigerator, and for the first time in more than a year I cooked a little meat and a fresh vegetable every night on my old kerosene wick burner or Coleman stove. Architecturally, the new home reminded me of a prison cell block. I missed the soothing woven bamboo walls and as soon as possible covered walls with woven grass *imbe* and black-and-white handpainted *massi* cloth made from mulberry bark. I made curtains and bought a small electric fan for bedside use. Not the Taj Mahal, but functional and clean.

One day a starved abandoned kitten walked forlornly through the agricultural office, so I bought cat food and got on the bus with a frightened kitten's head showing out the top of my knapsack. Using a drop of my own insecticide, I carefully encircled the kitten's neck, and the next day the kitten was without fleas and curled up on my bed. She was the best substitute for insecticide and mouse poison. Only a month later she was busy chasing and eating mice and cockroaches and leaving various body parts scattered around the apartment.

There was soon to be one more addition to my domestic scene. On a Saturday, opening my back door to hang out laundry, I frightened an emaciated young white dog slinking along the concrete trench under my apartment kitchen. When I finished my dishes, opening the drain, the water ran outside into a ditch and eventually into a sewer flowing into the Rewa River across the street. The dog was sniffing out bits of food from kitchen sinks emptying from inside all the apartments.

The small dog had the sharp, pointed head of all semi-wild Fijian dogs and was covered with faint gray spots as if a housepainter had splashed him with a dirty brush. It was not a puppy but not yet fully grown and limping badly. I brought some bread and milk to him, but the dog would not come to the dish. He desperately wanted the food. Holding his head and neck submissively, he crouched, and his stringy tail thumped hard against the ground. His need for food did not win over his expectation of a hurtful kick. Finally, I put the bowl on the doorstep, closed the door, and went inside. Soon there was the sound of a dog lapping up the milk. By Monday morning the dog was mine. I named him *Koli Lailai*, for Dog Little.

A few weeks later *Koli Lailai* was brave enough to leave the back door area, follow me to the bus stop and wait with me. I boarded the bus and sat down in my seat, and fellow passengers started yelling and I found *Koli Lailai* hiding under my seat. I carried him off the bus and reboarded.

One evening after supper, I was reading the daily newspaper, when a loud knock on my front door surprised me. All the windows were low, and whoever was outside could see me. I opened the door to the giant black Police Chief Sekovi, who had more than a year ago paid a courtesy visit to me up in the bush. Even in this full-sized doorway he stooped to enter.

Sekovi smiled broadly and said, "I'm visiting family in my village down the road and I took the opportunity to visit you. How are you doing?"

"Managing well. Come in and have a seat. Last time you visited me we sat on the floor of my little *bure*. Tonight I can offer you a chair."

Sekovi was a man who was fully aware of his great size. He glanced at the fragile government issue desk chair and lowered himself in slow motion. He never tried to shift the chair closer to the dining table. His appraisal was correct; we both heard a suspicious squeak. He put both elbows on the sturdier table and made an effort to take some of the load off the chair. He glanced at my drink.

"Sekovi, how would you like a little Scotch and water? Sorry, no ice. My refrigerator doesn't make any."

"That would be welcome."

I brought him his drink and sat down at the table across from him. "Sekovi, I still don't have any marijuana to share with you and this time also no cigarette. I hope this will suffice."

This was one cool police chief. He smiled at me and said, "To your health, Barbara, to your long life and good health and also to your *bulamacows*."

We clinked our glasses together to finalize the toast, but before I could take a sip the smile on his face vanished and he said, "You hold your glass higher than mine, Barbara, this is an insult to me. Your glass must always be lower than mine when touching, just as your head must always be lower than mine."

I struggled not to laugh. He was not in the least seeing any humor in what he said. He was almost two feet taller than I was. I would have to climb a chair to meet him eye to eye. This man was serious. He actually looked as if he had been slapped. At that moment I knew this was not a courtesy visit. There was another reason why he came. I hardly needed a police chief angry with me. I suggested a toast of my own, an equal one of health and long life to him, and with my glass touching only the base of his. His face relaxed and we drank.

Our conversation, vapid on his part, polite on mine, lasted only long enough for him to drain his glass. He soon left. His visit was a puzzle to me, and an unpleasant one at that.

Within a few days after moving into town, I found heavy gauge metal fencing in a work shed and, using my heaviest nails, completely covered all the windows.

I wasn't the only civil servant living in fear. Richard stopped at my desk one morning. His usual severe expression softened, and he hesitated before he spoke.

"Barbara, my wife and I think it best you move into our home with us and our children."

This was the first time he had shown me any kind of humanity, anything other than his crisp British politeness.

For a moment I was incapable of saying anything. I scrutinized his face. "Richard, surely that is not necessary. My government housing is good enough. I have a shower and electricity. This is luxury to a bush dweller. Not pretty, but quite civilized."

"In that case, you should have a housegirl live with you. You shouldn't live alone. A Fijian girl would be best."

"Yes. I can manage to bring one of Maria's older daughters to live with me. Be sure to thank your wife for me. Would you care to tell me what made you ask?"

"Looks like Beni is living in town and he's been drinking. Again, that is. Most Fijian men can't handle alcohol."

"I've heard that—many times—they go a little crazy when they drink and don't stop until out of control. Is he still working for the Ministry of Agriculture?"

"Stevens hasn't decided what to do with Beni for the time being. He's on half-pay for now. He will have to be reassigned into another region. Stevens sent one of the newly graduated Fijian men up to your scheme, and when Beni found out he went on a drunken rampage."

If I was ever going to tell Richard about my near-truck accident it had to be at that time. But what exactly were the facts? Swear under oath it was Beni? The close call took only a matter of seconds. There was always a possibility my anxiety had run amok. Richard guessed there was something I wanted to say. He waited a moment before he turned briskly away and back to his office.

Now, in town with Indian and Fijian civil servant neighbors close by in adjacent apartments, Richard was suddenly alarmed for my safety. I tried to convince myself that he was overreacting. Beni was out of work. Where was he? What was he doing? Still driving the red Buick taxi in the city, licensed to an Indian? Possibly still trucking diseased cattle from one region to the other, buying wholesale and selling retail? Working for the Hungarian lumber czar? He now had lost his leverage with Laszlo. Beni was no longer a civil servant working a cattle operation with grade-one virgin hardwood. How was he going to replace all the farmers' money he never banked? Beni had also lost his free government housing and the steady income of a civil servant.

Where was Beni's home village? No one I asked knew where he had been born or who his parents and family were. In Fiji, people without a village to call home, people who are shunned by their families, can be seen sleeping on park benches. Was Beni one more case of persona non grata?

The village culture is a forgiving one, but there is a limit. A chiefly son in a neighboring village wrecked the school bus twice before he was replaced. Both times he was drunk. Why was he not fired after the first accident? An aunt of his said, "We all can make a mistake once." She also said that if her nephew didn't change his ways he would be shunned by his village and cast out permanently.

A shunned Fijian moves into a town for work, and if he is unskilled he will soon be seen drunk and sleeping on a bench somewhere. After some months if he has been able to find work, and alcohol hasn't destroyed him, he may return to his village and hope the elders will take him back. If the village is economically a healthy one, he has a chance, but he will have lost face, which is a form of forever being on probation.

No one I questioned had a clue as to where Beni's birth village was. He was homeless. That alone was alarming news. He had obviously been permanently shunned by his birth village for some egregious and unforgivable act.

The office scuttlebutt said Beni had an associate's degree and Stevens was trying to relocate him into one of the other three agricultural regions. For all of our sakes I wished Beni Godspeed.

I remembered the warning given me during orientation week a year ago: be wary of going *tropo*. Here was Stevens resorting to village mentality. He and Richard had finally studied my farm reports. They had proof of embezzlement and movement of sick cattle onto the scheme. Instead of using the country's courts, Stevens was giving Beni another chance. Would his new superior be apprised of his new livestock officer's history? Another unspoken question.

18
Timoci

Working at HQ one afternoon, I looked up from my paperwork and into the beaming face of my language instructor, Timoci. After leaving his classes more than a year ago I had lost track of him. No longer wearing a carelessly wrapped old *sulu* tied around his waist, he was wearing tailored slacks, a white shirt, and new shoes.

"Barbara, why is my very own worst language student sitting behind a desk in HQ? No chasing *bulamacows* anymore?"

"Timoci, *bula, bula*. For goodness' sake, what are you doing here?"

"Picking up some reports for my father. He doesn't like leaving his village anymore. He's getting old and cranky."

"You're going to be in town awhile?"

"For two days. That's all. Then the U.S. Embassy is sending me to London for leadership training. After that I go to the USA. Your country. Miss Marian at the Embassy found United Nations money for me."

"Very exciting; you have to tell me all about it. How about tomorrow night, a Suva restaurant, my treat, a going-away party, OK?"

More than a year ago Timoci, our Fijian language teacher, had come to our classes with a briefcase in one hand and a battered Gibson guitar in the other. We never saw this young, handsome six-footer without a huge beguiling smile on his face. We were never strangers to him. His fun-loving personality was irresistible. When we stumbled over his language, making perfect fools out of ourselves conversing with him in Fijian, he might look puzzled at times but never made us feel like adult imbeciles.

My last assignment, a final written test he gave me on the spur of the moment, was to explain my mission in Fiji. It was the only time Timoci laughed uproariously and with such gusto his laugh was contagious and he did not embarrass me. My essay, translated into Fijian, told of educating twenty-one eager but inexperienced cattle farmers in the management of cattle while running naked through their 3,000-acre cattle scheme.

Evenings after long days of grammar lessons, we relaxed with Fiji Bitters Beer. Timoci brought his guitar and entertained us with a Fijian's version of Elvis Presley singing "All Shook Up," "Love Me Tender," and other ballads. With his low-down gyrating hips he had no idea how funny he was. He enjoyed life, loved to dance, and had an insatiable curiosity about all American popular music. None of us found out until later that Timoci was destined, after the death of his father, to be an important *turanga*, a chief from one of the larger islands with a strong and stable agricultural base. We did suspect that Timoci was being prepared for a future that did not include teaching his language to many more itinerant expatriates.

During dinner Timoci took a long drink of his Fiji Bitters Beer and said, "Bags packed, not one *sulu* or even a pair of sandals inside. A raincoat I've never worn, a lined windbreaker that makes me feel like I want to tear it off and shred it. Barbara, I don't know if I can think with all these heavy clothes on. And I don't want to leave my country. I've never even been way from my village for more than a few weeks."

His smile vanished as he spoke. The carefree young man was now apprehensive and homesick while he was still in his own country. In two days, cold, drizzly London would become his home for six months. The Timoci known for this life of fun, his practiced easy flirting with Fijian girls, was leaving for a country from which his father had worked all his life to gain freedom. Timoci was the firstborn son of a *turanga*, well educated, and as was obvious to everyone who ever met him, very intelligent. Now his elderly father was in failing health and Timoci's own frivolous ways were coming to an end.

He looked thoroughly miserable. He reached for my hand for comfort, and I let my hand remain under his. My emotions were similar to the day I sent my firstborn off to college. I felt all the same anxieties plus many more. Timoci was going to be overwhelmed with culture shock, the only Fijian in a tight-upper-lip society holding onto their class structure with a bulldog death grip. He would be treated with disrespect; he would see himself as a stranger. He had been born into a culture that had only two categories: family and stranger. He would begin to question his self-worth. He was headed for dangers without the tools to survive.

During dinner I had been subliminally aware of hostile glances from diners adjacent to our table. One of the two middle-aged women was obviously a British aristocrat, and the other sounded American. Conversation between Timoci and me was their only concern. When we spoke, the two women stopped talking, pushed food around their plates, and leaned their heads delicately toward our table. Timoci's bemused expression led me to write on a notepad: "Who are those horrid busybodies?" He wrote back: "The American ambassador's wife and the British ambassador's wife."

I found myself suddenly peering at Timoci from the point of view of British and American elite, and yes indeed, these women might well be curious. He was tall and slender, his skin color more copper brown than black, and handsome by all universal standards. He wore new casual clothing for his journey, and his manners were easy but correct. Only his race and his thick halo of African hair placed him outside their culture. He was also the same age as my youngest child.

In a clear, loud voice I exclaimed. "Timoci, you may find having dinner with a white woman in London and in New York City and certainly Paris will cause far less of a stir than in your very own country! You may take my word for it."

Timoci failed to restrain himself. He spoke loudly enough for our neighbors to hear, "I certainly hope so. The British want to hold us back, and the Americans like you, Barbara, push and shove and tease us toward a working democracy. There are times I wish you would all return to your own countries and leave us to our own destiny."

He didn't stop there. He watched as one of the women's linen napkins slid to the floor. He rose, picked it up, bowed stiffly, and, mimicking the King's English, said, "Permit me, madam, one last act of subservience."

The American lady's response was somewhere between a surprised snicker and a giggle. The British lady never hesitated before she spoke.

"Young man, you go too far. Yes indeed, too far."

Shortly, the two women left the restaurant.

"Do you think you went too far, Timoci?"

"I'm still in my country. No, I didn't go too far. In twenty-four hours, when I'm in that woman's country, well

... then I will have to work very hard at not going too far, won't I?"

"How hard are you going to try, I wonder? Marian at the embassy will be getting progress reports on you. She expects you to come back a polished diplomat, a smooth operator, a *turanga* who can bring a healthy economy to your new country."

"Barbara, often we Fijians disagree among ourselves. We have a thousand-year-old village culture. It's a good, strong culture, a healthy one. But we rely too much on the tourist industry, our rain forests are being timbered too fast, and our agricultural programs are hindered by incompetence. We behave ourselves in our villages, but in our cities ... well, in our cities we become rebellious and lose control of ourselves."

"Did you mean it, Timoci? You wish we would all leave your country and let you solve your problems in your own way?"

"Of course I do. I also admit it may be too soon. I know it is too soon."

"If you understand the vital part your country played in the victory over the Japanese in World War II, you will understand why our Pentagon will never take its eyes off your country and neither will the Brits. It appears you are stuck with us."

"The *turangas*, most of them dead now, voted to help train your soldiers in jungle warfare. The chiefs permitted you to build one of the largest airfields in the Pacific in Nandi for your bombers and fighters. We helped build a bridge to your battles on Japanese islands."

"Somehow, Timoci, you will also learn to bridge village and city. To build a more diverse economy. You will have to. Without progress, where are you?"

Timoci smiled, his eyes alive with amusement. "The American *bulamacow* lady built a bridge to healthy fat cows and healthy calves while running nude over three thousand acres. Yes, that is what I think."

"Not without many painful casualties. I'm not the trusting *bulamacow* lady I was when you first tried to teach me your language."

"Thank God you are a better *bulamacow* lady then you were a pupil. You have a reputation for speaking my language with what is described as an ingrown tongue. Did I teach you that, too?"

"What you did teach all of us was to like your people. That was more important. I still like your people, but not your tropical diseases. Also, I don't like that you and the Indians can't get along together. One hundred years and you still can't manage to accept each other."

"Barbara, we have four races and four cultures in our country. On our world map we are nothing more than two hundred tiny dots along with two larger islands. Sometimes I fear chaos between the races will lead to bloodshed on our islands."

"This is why the U.S. Embassy is sending you to London tomorrow. You will find a way, but you will not find it here in your own country, not here; you must leave."

"We've been independent from the British for more than a decade, and our new freedom has brought us more chaos and not less. The Indians resent our independence. Yes, I can see this. I can also see that I am too afraid that the perfect order and tranquillity of our villages will bring us only stagnation."

Outside the restaurant Timoci and I shook hands. He was getting too serious again.

"In my village we do not easily say farewell when we know we will never see each other again. It is final, like a death. In times past, at parting, we performed a ceremony similar to a ceremony of death. But sometimes if we loved the person very much the parting ceremony would go on for days with much *yanqona* drinking."

"I know your grog ceremonies all too well. Almost did me in when I fell insensate into one of your *yanqona tanoa* bowls. I much prefer American good-bye parties. I can more easily keep count of my drinks. With your grog, five is not enough and ten is too much."

"Maybe we drink *yanqona* until we are what you call insensate so we do not feel so sad when we say good-bye. Yes, that is what I think."

"Be sure to buy warm clothes in London. It's winter there now, your very first winter of your life. Good-bye, Timoci; take care of yourself so you can come back and be the best *turanga* in your country."

Under the streetlight I saw Timoci's eyes shimmer behind tears. Saying good-bye was as hard as seeing my children leave for college. Harder, because I knew I would never see him again. I quickly turned and walked away, fighting the urge to look back.

19
The Future—An Unwelcome Guest

Marian and I sat on her balcony with a view of a tranquil aquamarine sea. Although she referred to herself as only the number-two U.S. Embassy Consul, Marian lived in a new and opulent two-story home with all the modern trappings and a live-in Fijian housekeeper.

"Barbara, we rarely know how we feel about someone until we learn we will never see them again. You were the best person for Timoci to spend his last evening with. Until he got on that plane this morning I didn't know if he would actually leave. He was downright frightened."

I shouldn't have been surprised that Marian knew about my dinner with Timoci. In Suva, a white woman, dining alone with a good-looking young Fijian man did not go unnoticed. I shouldn't have been surprised, but I was. I made an effort not to show my annoyance. The Scotch was smooth, dinner was sending us delicious aromas, and I wanted to be a pleasant companion. I let my eyes rest on the sea, hoping for a crimson-orbed tropical sunset.

"Thank God I live the life of a nun, if an irreverent nun," I finally said. "Gossip in Suva and gossip via the jungle grapevine in the bush move with the speed of light."

Marian smiled wanly. "Wives of embassy personnel get bored to death, no TV, no soaps, no museums, no concerts, no jobs. The women release stress by gossiping. I can even tell you what you had for dinner, how you dressed and how many beers you bought Timoci, and one or two other little tidbits."

"With women like that, our taxpayers don't have to pay your spooks, your shadowy men in cloaks, assigned to watch over your embassy."

"Ah, but they do. My phone is tapped. When you call your taxi later you'll get several seconds of static before the call can go through."

"Good heavens! You can't have a personal life?"

"Not without constant scrutiny, never. At first it got to me. Then I had my little sailboat shipped to me. It's berthed at the Suva Yacht Club. Something about sailing on a day with a gentle breeze—cares and frustrations fall way."

"You've learned to trim your sails on land and on sea. Still, it must be frustrating—no intimate relationships, no close friends. You can't take your sailboat to bed with you, can you? How many more years before you go back home?"

"Five more years, that's all. I can hold it together for that long."

"Well, you're not exactly living in a slum, Marian. If this is the level of government housing for a USA Embassy Consul, the lady who enjoyed gossiping about me last night must live in a palace."

"Ah, but being number two isn't enough for me. I was number one before I got to Fiji. And I've had to pay a price for this level."

"You haven't been here very long?"

"In my last post, in a country our State Department considers vital for maintaining military bases, well... something happened.... Who knows? Perhaps I was there too long."

"They call it going *tropo*, don't they?"

Marian looked sideways at me and chose not to answer. Instead she took our drinks, went into the kitchen, and poured us another round.

"Marian, when Timoci comes home again how will he see his country?"

"At first he'll want to change everything. After a year or two? I don't know. That's a tough one. Will he get used to the smelly *vale lailai* again and the torpid rhythm of his old village?"

"Will he go back to teaching Fijian to expatriates?"

"With the money we're investing in him we expect a lot more from him. He'll soon be the new chief, later the *turanqa* of his island, and he will take his place in the Fijian Council of Chiefs."

"After London and New York, will Timoci be content officiating at the *yanqona* bowl?"

"Hard to tell. He's intelligent and I expect him to be ambitious. But we can't ever really be certain. During my student days at Radcliffe I roomed with a scholarship student from Appalachia. Brilliant girl. At our tenth year reunion, the whole class showed up but not my roommate; she was back in the hills living in a shack made out of piano crates covered with tarpaper."

"Not even teaching?"

"No one knew what she was doing with her life."

"What a waste."

"Just about the best education a woman can get in our country." Marian continued, "I suspect she wasn't equipped to confront her Appalachian families. A case of her desperate need to reduce dissonance. It was more important for her to be accepted by her family than it was to change values. I admit I worry about Timoci. Will he do any better than my roommate? I call it my piano crate syndrome."

"I've never lived in a piano crate, but a bamboo *bure* with a thatch roof, surrounded by other *bures*, can be quite cozy. Someday you might try it."

"Have we lost you too, Barbara?"

"If only we had plumbing in a *bure* I might be tempted."

"The village way of life, it's a cocoon. Safe; the spirit of competition is an evil thing, a taboo. How can you breathe in that atmosphere?"

"Marian, I felt cared for in my village. No, I didn't feel loved but watched over as a child is watched over. Yes, I felt safe. I loved feeling safe. But then something happened and I had to leave. And here in the city I'm always on guard."

"Feeling safe, being accepted, was more important to you than properly managing a sick cattle herd?"

"Not in the end. No. Making that decision—well, it cost me. When, I, *bulamacow* lady, finally used whatever cutting edge I had to expose Beni, I broke totally with the village way of dealing with deceit. I felt sick inside. A little like a traitor."

"And you moved out of the bush and into town."

"But I left voluntarily, Marian. No one asked me to leave. Not like I was shunned or banished. That was very important to me."

"Why, then, did you leave?"

"I was sick. Some kind of tropical disease. There are many undiagnosed tropical diseases, no cures, no medicines; you know that."

"You had the option to move back to your scheme after you were well again."

This woman, this embassy lady, was never not working. She lit a cigarette, lay back on her chaise longue, and gazed silently out to sea. I got up from my chair, stretched out my arms, and wished Marian didn't ask such hard questions. On her desk she kept a folder of my work, my activities, my life here. It was her job. Surely she must guess why I couldn't go back.

With my elbows leaning on the balcony rail I looked across the street at a newly built house, not quite as luxurious as Marian's but by *bure*-in-a-village standard a livable, attractive house. Marian, had told me earlier she was fairly certain the embassy spook lived across the street. He would have to be white. I couldn't imagine a Fijian having the motivation for low-level spy work or any covert surveillance.

How could I explain to Marian the duplicity Beni exhibited in his life? How dim-witted and slow I was to comprehend and finally to accept the fact that it was my job to expose him; how he involved his superiors in his chicanery to guarantee their protection? How had he involved Stevens? Possibly he sold him cheap but diseased cattle for his own ranch? As a vet, Stevens would have been too embarrassed to go public. Being persona non grata in his birth country, this man would spend the rest of his life vulnerable.

Suni? How did Beni buy Suni's loyalty? That was easy to answer; he took the rap, instead of a drunk Suni, for running down the Indian woman who later died. Richard? Beni probably had not been able to corrupt Richard, yet. Perhaps Beni was able to frighten him, a family man with young children. None of this information was something I cared to discuss with a high-ranking embassy lady. For whatever reason, Marian herself was under surveillance. It came with her job. For a career diplomat this was just one more day at the office.

I turned around and faced Marian. "You're right; I could have returned to the scheme. I exposed corruption, but not to give vent to my competitive spirit. Because the health of the farmers was in danger. As simplistic as this is, the distinction is too abstract for Beni. He saw only his loss of power, his loss of money. He responded by losing control of himself."

"Beni was a casualty in the making. No one knows how to handle him. Predictably he's a hybrid. Won't be confined by village culture and can't stay clean in the city."

We both watched as the sun grew in size and dipped into the sea. The silence between us was a welcome one. Just as the sun dropped from view, a fan of fire rippled across the water toward us. On the horizon the color of the sea turned cobalt blue and toward the beach shaded down to a turquoise. In the bush sunset quickly plunged me into night with a scramble for insecticides or a fast retreat under a mosquito net. Here in the city people responded to a lovely sunset with languor and nostalgia. A good day or a stressful one, we lose ourselves in a few moments of splendor. Tomorrow is on hold. Tomorrow is irrelevant.

Marian stood up and asked, "I'm having my last drink for the evening. Do you want another?"

"A small one, please."

When Marian returned with the drinks, I asked, "How is Timoci going to respond to living in London and in the States? If he loses that strong sense of belonging to his village, he may lose everything. He might begin to wonder if he has anything to live for."

"He's looking forward to it. He told me he wants to bring TV to Fiji. He wants to bring the Western world to his country."

TV in this country, birthed by volcanoes, was an incredible and silly notion to me. "TV in the villages? Is that his horizon, his ambition? I also haven't seen electricity in any of the villages." I continued, "Did he specify soap opera or the Metropolitan Opera?"

Marian avoided my sarcasm. "He mentioned hydroelectric plants. He will learn to talk to men and women holding foreign venture capital for economic development. The decision to bring TV or any industry to Fiji will be made by him, the other chiefs, and of course the Indian businessmen."

"The heart of this and all the other third world nations lies in its villages," I said. "TV in an ancient culture will destroy it."

"Will it? These villages are living in a time warp."

Our voices were getting strident and brittle. "It's a time warp that keeps their people safe and out of harm's way," I snapped back at Marian.

"Barbara, you've gone *tropo* on us. Once you get back to the States you'll think a lot more clearly. Fiji has to move forward. Do you know how high the rate of illiteracy is? TV can also be used constructively."

Marian shifted uneasily in her lounge chair. She lit a cigarette from the stub of her dying one. I almost enjoyed feeling her discomfort.

"Timoci's father, the *turanga*, showed up unannounced at the U.S. Embassy a few months ago. He asked me to send his son to leadership training. To teach him democratic theory. Ironic; did you know that in the late eighteen hundreds King Cakobau, an enthusiastic cannibal, first asked the USA to accept his country as a colony? His offer was rejected, so he went to Queen Victoria, who thought it a mighty fine idea."

"So it was Timoci's father who made the decision to send his son to leadership training."

"Timoci has little choice but to obey his father. I am also concerned with Josete's innocence, his childlike curiosity, his naive trust, his leaving his village cocoon. Not an easy decision for me."

I was having a hard time keeping sarcasm in check. "At heart you're a real softy, Marian, right?"

"Admit? Never!" There was anger in her voice. "Those spooks keep me on alert."

Finding that Marian was just as vulnerable in her high-level foreign service job as all the civil servants I was working with was for me demoralizing. I needed to feel that Marian, a fellow American I admired and respected, never felt vulnerable and had nothing in her past to compromise her career. But for some reason she had opened herself up to me just enough for me to understand that she needed to protect herself. I was only vaguely sorry to have challenged her.

"Don't worry too much about Timoci's innocence," I said. "During language classes we gave him a healthy dose of our culture. Maybe more than he knows. By the end of our first week of classes we had taught him to sing in Fijian 'Happiness Is a Thing Called Joe.' By the end of our three-week classes, during an all-night Fiji Bitters Beer party, we taught him in Fijian, Louis Armstrong's version of 'Bow-legged Woman.' We told him ol' Satchmo would approve."

Marian laughed and said, "I question your idea of a healthy dose of Americana. Is there a word for 'bowlegged woman' in the Fijian dictionary?"

"Not in this context. The dictionary translates *bowed* into *crooked*. Timoci asked why someone would write a song about a man wanting a woman with crooked legs? We told him it was purely a cultural thing in America.

Something like Fijians' enjoying drinking *yanqona*. Something unexplainable. He thanked us and said he would try to remember this when he came to the States. He would always first look for a pretty woman with crooked legs."

"I got that young man away from your corrupting influence barely in time." Marian laughed. I think she was trying to forgive me for challenging her competency.

"He can be elegant and diplomatic," I said. "I wouldn't be a bit surprised if he humored his American students. He enjoyed our little jokes. When he comes home, ask him if he dated any women with crooked legs."

"First, you may be sure, there will be other questions for him."

"By then he will have had his first look at a world that has used and misused his island nation. First by the Dutch, then by Captain Cook and Bligh, then as a British colony and, before he was born, the Americans during World War II."

"During World War II, the Allies had no choice. This country was vital to military strategies. But it was the beginning of Fiji getting global attention."

"For Timoci and his young friends, Marian, that was another time, another world. Today, does Timoci understand why you're here, why I'm here, why our cunning Laszlo and his lumbermill are all here, why—?"

Marian interrupted, "I'm also thinking of sending him to Calcutta. After he has had a glimpse and a whiff of Calcutta will he know how to handle the Indian problem here? Will he then know why the Indians won't or can't go home?"

"Perhaps. Or perhaps he'll remind them they arrived, low-caste indentured servants, in filthy British transport ships and that now they are free and have money. Now they should get on a nice clean jumbo jet and go home."

Marian laughed and said, "Wouldn't that be lovely. I have a friend in the Pentagon who never misses each and every opportunity to remind me that not one Indian fought or helped the Allies during World War II. He is convinced they are all closet communists."

"And the Fijians?"

"He rather likes them. The general was a private during the war. He learned jungle warfare from them. He credits them with saving his young life. He remembers one old chief, who was a child during earlier days of cannibalistic rites, he told my friend to never leave a Japanese prisoner alive."

"Sounds a bit harsh."

Marian raised her eyebrows and said, "Not to a Fijian. Their concept of imprisonment is far more cruel than instant death by machete. It's the old 'tough-gentle' way of looking at life. In this culture, people live only for today. Their idea of the future is ambiguous. In prison a lot of men quickly become mentally deranged. Only the Indian prisoners are assured of their afterlife."

"Timoci is so gentle, so kind. Still I know he is only two generations away from . . ."

Marian watched me as my voice faded into silence. Finally I said, "I am fearful for him. His father is ill and very old. He may never see his father again."

"He probably won't; that is why the *turanga* came to see me. Josete entered our United Nations leadership training program knowing he can't return until he has completed his studies. Not even for his father's funeral. Not for any reason. No nonscheduled flights back home."

"When he returns he'll sit on the Fijian Council of Chiefs. Will the old men accept his ideas? He is now touched, even tainted, by foreign cultures."

"In the eyes of the old men?" Marian continued. "I don't know. He's going to attend workshops in India. Timoci almost backed out when I told him he would be living for a short time as a guest in the home of an Indian lawyer in the Indian Parliament. At that very moment I fully expected to lose him to our program."

"If the lawyer has one of those young daughters of flawless beauty that I see here in Fiji, our stiff-necked and lonely prince may very well lose his heart and bend a little."

"Barbara, away from his home for the first time in his life anything is possible, but have you ever seen a Fijian and an Indian in an intimate relationship?"

"Never. Also, Timoci is spoken for. He and his third cousin, the daughter of a chiefly family, are betrothed."

"He didn't volunteer this information to me. You and he are close friends, aren't you?"

"Not in our cultural definition of friends. No, not at all. No. There's no category for friend. There is only family or stranger. He and I are friendly, but there is a difference. This difference is a foot-thick wall between us."

"Eventually there must be one more category. How can governments function within this paradigm?"

"This wall between Timoci and me becomes a ten-foot-thick wall between him and the Indians. Timoci and I respect each other. He does not respect Indians. One hundred years of living together, and they do not share respect."

"I've seen this. Every year the embassy organizes roundtable dialogues between Fijian and Indian leaders. We hear only polite rehearsed speeches."

"In this country words unspoken are the most lethal. The silent words, they frighten me the most."

"Barbara, it is very hard for me to imagine anything frightens or intimidates you more than five minutes."

"Now that I am no longer under the protection of the old chief on my cattle scheme, the one who announced that he had adopted me as his daughter, yes, I am often uneasy."

"But you are now living in government housing in town. Indians and Fijians are your neighbors. Surely you are safer here than deep in the bush and alone."

"Not at all. In the village I was family; I was a daughter to a chief. His protection was not an illusion. Here in town I am a stranger without a family. Sometimes I do feel shunned. It's not a good feeling. I miss the feeling of belonging. In that way, yes, I admit I've gone *tropo*."

Marian waited a moment before she said quietly, "Your passport is in my safe whenever you want it."

20
The Ancients Come Knocking

The Indian taxi driver, the same one Marian always used for her commute to the embassy, picked me up at her house at ten o'clock that night. I felt safe with him driving through dark, nearly empty Suva streets and into the more isolated area of my apartment housing. The driver stopped his car near the entrance to the compound, and as I walked to my unit I was woefully aware of the total blackness surrounding me—no streetlights, windows dark, all the other civil service employees gone to bed. The apartment compound was as dark as the bush in the hills on a moonless night. And where was my Koli Lei Lei? He must be hungry for his dinner. Usually as soon as I entered the compound he ran to me from under my apartment, where he had dug himself a cool cave.

I got my pen-sized flashlight out as I walked around to the rear of the apartments. The back door had a sturdy padlock, which I always kept locked. The front door was flimsy, and I usually jammed a chair back under the doorknob and locked the door from the inside.

I inserted the key into the padlock and lifted it off, but when I turned the doorknob I found it covered with a thick sticky substance. I opened the door and stepped over the threshold, and then a stiff, bulky object brushed against my forehead. I pulled the chain of the ceiling light and in its cold glare found my kitten hanging upside-down on the outside of the door. She was nailed by the base of her tail to the wood planks. Blood running down the full length of her body had congealed on her face. Blood dripping down the door had formed a soft, gummy gel on the steps. I froze motionless staring at her. Her mouth agape, fangs exposed, lips pulled tight, the cat's grimace in death looked nothing like the soft, cuddly kitten I had left curled up on my steps that morning.

I finally closed the door and locked it from the inside. Who would do such a thing? Was the kitten dead before being nailed to the door? She must have been, or the Indian neighbors sharing the wall of my apartment would have heard her cries. I knew Indians were passive in their feeling about pets, but they would never be so cruel. Never.

Was my kitten nailed to my door by someone who knew I never used the front door? Might it be a Fijian living in the compound or someone who had been watching me from the heavily forested hills behind my apartment? The grassy area below the hill was where I hung up my laundry or sat and played with Koli Lei Lei and the kitten.

I had little contact with any of my neighbors, Fijian or Indian. After work I was too tired for any activity other than a shower, a simple meal, and to bed with a book. Whatever tropical disease had made me ill, it still had a hold on my immune system, only slowly losing its grip.

There was no reason for a neighbor to want to hurt me. None at all. And this was the clue. This was a message being sent. A warning. A warning with its roots in a two-thousand-year-old culture, from the days when tribal wars were as predictable as the rainy season.

Chief Siti's son, Kona, told me the story of his great-grandfather's last battle with another village during the days of incessant tribal warfare, before Fiji became a British colony. Many long sessions of two chiefs of two villages had not solved a question of boundary. One morning, Kona's great-grandfather found a large dead bat tied to the thatch roof of his *bure*. The message was clear: "You and your villagers have three days to leave your *mataqali* land or we will attack."

The tribal battle began on the third day and ended with Kona's great-grandfather the victor. The slain chief's body was brought to the village. The in-ground *lovo* ovens were fired up, and during a long night of celebrating one of the last cannibalistic feasts took place. The ceremonial *tanoa* bowl was kept filled with *yanqona* until daybreak.

Could this bizarre and pagan warning have any weight today? Today in a Christian twentieth-century world? I told myself nothing more would happen that night. If this was a warning, I needed to take action but not tonight. I tried hard to convince myself of that singular fact. Tomorrow morning I would make a decision. For now I felt it necessary to bury the kitten before all species of insects attacked the corpse and eventually my apartment.

My kitten was dead, beyond feeling pain. However she was removed, either by pulling her off the door or by using the small crowbar to remove the nail, neither would inflict more pain. Before I was aware of it, I started whispering to myself. I was regressing to habits of my childhood. When truly stressed I always whispered to myself, hoping no one would hear.

"Be sensible. Bury your kitten as soon as possible—this will help put the entire gory scene to rest. In the morning . . . plant something pretty on the grave. Bury the kitten tonight or the Indian children next door will also see the gruesome scene on their way to school. No need to frighten innocent children. Just do it and stop all this whining."

I tried to remember where I had seen my small hand shovel and looked in closets and kitchen cabinets. I finally found the shovel behind Koli Lei Lei's dog food bag. Where was he? This was not like him at all—by now he should be eating his dinner.

I started digging in a brushy area close enough to the back door so the light within the room gave me a bit of help. While digging I considered the fact that both Indians and Fijians really are not into the pet mind-mode. Not like the English and Americans. In this country pets were synonymous with pests. Disease-carrying varmints, that is how cats and dogs are perceived in the third world. Could it be a neighbor who had done this? But why the horror of nailing the kitten to my door? I still hoped my theory that it was a warning was an exaggeration, that jungle voodoo, jungle taboo, had taken an obsessive hold on me. I had not heeded the warnings given during orientation classes—beware, we are all vulnerable, especially when we are frightened.

Somewhere in the surrounding darkness I heard a rustling of leaves, and when I stood up to find from where the sounds came I heard the whimper of a dog close by. A slowly moving light gray dog came stumbling toward me, and I was relieved to find it was my Koli Lei Lei. I reached for him to comfort him and tell him dinnertime wasn't far away. Instead of coming to me, Koli Lei Lei hesitated and again whimpered. He finally came to me, and I reached out to stroke his head. I recoiled after feeling his head encrusted with what I thought was dirt, damp dirt. I coaxed Koli Lei Lei to the doorway of my apartment to get a better look at him. His head was bloodied and his jaw dripped with fresh blood. His lower jaw hung loose and swung against his blood-covered chest. His entire mandible was fully cracked from side to side; broken, it hung only by its skin.

* * *

The next day at HQ, Richard called one of the town's policemen to his office. The three of us drove to my apartment. During the drive Richard was strangely silent and the officer sat in the back of the Jeep and was stony-faced.

Richard administered a lethal drug by injection, and the whimpering Koli Lei Lei slipped into his final sleep. Under my hand his body relaxed and then he was gone. I quickly escaped to the shower room to be alone and compose myself.

This is a country of messages given in silence. Richard had refused to come near my apartment without a policeman. He never explained why the policeman was necessary but didn't really have to. The Fijian policeman stayed with us the entire time, silent but his eyes alert, and he never relaxed his stern expression. The decision I made was the only choice left to me.

While Richard and the policeman stood by the government Jeep I packed as much as I could in my two suitcases and one carry-all. I rolled up the best *massi* cloth and *imbe* to take home with me to the States. I stood in the doorway, scanning for anything left behind. Six months ago there had been no bars on the windows as there were now. The stark vacated concrete-block apartment looked even more like a prison cell than when I first arrived.

That night I moved into a small hotel for a few days waiting for air tickets to Hawaii and then on to the States. I thought about my friend Marian, the number-two USA

Embassy lady. What would she think when she relinquished my passport to the courier? Might she light a cigarette, go to her window, lean out a little, gauge wind direction from some smokestack in sight, and make a decision as to sailing her little red sailboat this day or, then again, maybe not? I thought that she might be relieved at my going home and that she knew a great deal more about the cultural ambiguities of Fiji than I could ever comprehend.

* * *

For several months after arriving home in the States I received short handwritten letters. I read the letters only out of respect for the writers. I was not able to answer my little family on the other side of my world—not quite yet. I hid the letters away in an inactive file labeled: "Correspondence—Miscellaneous." I was confident that the time would come—I had no idea when—that I would bring sense and find a meaning out of my *bulamacow* days. I told myself to have the faith to believe that some goodness had been left behind. If not that, then a few hours of whimsical storytelling around the *yanqona* bowl.

Dear Miss Barbara:

Principal Lania sends you her best wishes. When my baby girl was born Dr. Tomba said the baby was perfect. He said he knew who the father was. I do not know how Dr. Tomba knew who the father was. I did not tell him. Principal Lania did not tell him. He said it was good to have a girl so that I would not name it after the father. I have named the baby Barbara because when you came to speak to us in our village and I asked you if I should take *wai-ni-yava*, bush medicine to get rid of the baby, you said it was safer for me to have the baby.

After the baby was born I went back to my village. I didn't have enough milk to nurse the baby. Several of the women were still nursing their babies, and for the first month they all took turns nursing her. She is now fat and is taking her first steps. I love my baby very much.

Sa mothe,
Arlene

Dear Miss Barbara:

Our cow with the three tits had a heifer calf last month and we call her Barbara because when you found her mother wandering in many other herds you always knew she was ours and you would tell us where to find her and to bring her home. We do not know who the father is because she wanders away all the time. My mother says she tries now to grow your new wing beans that you said was good for us but they do not taste as good as what my mother grows in her *tei tei*.

My mother cannot write letters and wants me to tell you the new Livestock Officer Mele is just out of college and this is his first job. He is almost as good with cattle as you are but I don't think he likes them as much as you did. I did not tell my mother but I found him and my oldest sister looking into each other's eyes. You know what that means. Also my oldest brother should be married but he did not want to bring a wife into our *bure*. It is too small and there are so many of us. Now he is going to move into your *bure* as soon as he has a wife to cook for him.

I miss you,
Ili

Dear Barbara:

Bula! Bula! You did not tell me the sun does not shine in London. I am often sad and homesick for my island village. My father the *turanga* died and when I return I will sit on the Fijian Council of Chiefs. I attend classes in the day and try to study at night. In my government leadership classes are men and women from many countries.

There are many pretty women in London and I have seen a few of Satchmo's "crooked-legged women." None of them are as pretty as the girls on my island. When I go to New York City I will follow your suggestion and look again.

I am sad to learn about what happened to you and that you had to leave my country. You did not have good help. When I return to Fiji I will try to help to bring our country into the modern world. Our old tribal ways are bringing a sickness to us. When we leave our villages we bring the worst of our culture into the city and when we return to our village culture we bring the worst of the cities with us. Yes, that is what I think.

                    Most Respectfully,
                    Timoci

Epilogue

In 1987, Fijian Army Officer Sitiveni Rabuka and his soldiers led a coup against the Indian-dominated government. Rabuka suspended the constitution and proclaimed Fiji a republic, severing ties with the commonwealth. The military coup was a bloodless one.

Conflicts between Fijians and Indians continued with the Taukei extremist group petrol-bombing a few Indian businesses and communities.

In 1998, after a new constitution was signed, Prime Minister Rabuka was replaced by the Indian Mahendra Chaudhry, the first Indian to serve as prime minister. In 1999, The Great Council of Chiefs, indigenous leaders, is in a heated conflict with Chaudhry as Indians are being evicted from their expired leased lands.